THE ^ORIGINAL GOLF SCHOOL™ WAY

IMPROVING YOUR GAME WITH THE ACCELERATED TEACHING METHOD™

Jay Morelli
and
Jim Reichert
Photography by
Bruce Curtis

The Schoolhouse Press

The Schoolhouse Press
107 Orchard Road
Mt. Kisco, NY 10549
USA

The Schoolhouse Press and its Schoolhouse Design Logo are registered trademarks of Reichert Ventures Company.

Designed by ARLENE SCHLEIFER GOLDBRERG
Manufactured in China by Blaze IPI/Jade

Library of Congress Control Number : 2001116424

First edition 2001

10 9 8 7 6 5 4 3 2 1

For: Amy Horowitz, John, Margaret, Michael, and Mateo Morelli;
Raina Bourland; Stacy, Sydney, and Shane Reichert;
and Lorraine, Tim and Julie Gilligan

Acknowledgements:

Writing a book is daunting, exhausting, and rigorous. For their contributions, the authors gratefully acknowledge: the staff at the Plantation Inn and Golf Resort in Crystal River, Florida; the staff at the Mount Snow Golf Course in Mount Snow, Vermont; Sue Newell; Mark Aebli; John Meckstroth; Barry Reynolds; Dawn and Bill Tsetseranos; John Wheatley; the Florida State golf team and Ann Giacomozzi; Peter Platt; David Reichert; Mark Shafer; Louise Reichert; Larry Feldstein; and most important, the more than 80,000 students and alumni of The *Original* Golf School™.

Table of Contents

Foreword by Hubert Green

I have known Jay Morelli since we played together on the Florida State University golf team. He has always had an outstanding command of the technical aspects of golf and over the years has deepened his understanding of the sport and perfected his methodology. He founded The *Original* Golf School™ with one goal—to teach his groundbreaking system, called The Accelerated Teaching Method™, to interested golfers. Over the years he has tutored more than 80,000 students, ranging from PGA professionals to first-timers.

The principles that Jay teaches can be applied by all golfers regardless of their skill level. No matter if you are a beginner or a PGA Grand Slam champion, if you are a golfer, you are continually struggling with your grip, stance, alignment and swing, short and long games, putting, etc. Golf is a sport that requires lifelong-learning, and through this clear, easy-to-read, book Jay can now be your golf guru.

I have benefited from knowing Jay, and have deepened my understanding of my own game through him. I think you and your game will benefit, too; regardless of your skill level. In fact, the only thing better for your game than reading this book would be to go to Jay's school.

Hubert Green is a U.S. Open Champion, PGA Champion, 17 PGA Tour victories, and is currently playing on the Senior PGA Tour.

Introduction by Jay Morelli

I love the game of golf. I am passionate about the game of golf. The happiest memories in my life are of playing golf with my father, John, and my son, Michael. However, for as wonderful as the game of golf can be, I also know that it can be maddeningly bewildering, and so confounding that the joys of the sport—being outside, breathing fresh air, and getting exercise with friends and family—can sometimes be overshadowed by frustration. I know that to really enjoy golf, a player must feel that he is playing to or near the best of his ability level.

I developed The Accelerated Teaching Method™ because I felt it was the best way to teach golfers of all levels how to really improve their knowledge of the sport of golf. The Accelerated Teaching Method™ starts beginning golfers on the green, close to the hole with short strokes. Then, by gradually moving further from the hole, a fuller, more complete swing is more easily actualized. For intermediate and advanced players, we utilize the concept of "strength enhancement" where we build upon what's right with each student's game.

At The *Original* Golf School™, we offer a low 4 to 1 student to pro ratio, meaning that each student receives plenty of personal attention and gets video analysis. Our small groups allow us to offer specialized programs for players at any level. Since 1978, more than 80,000 students have learned to play better golf and get more enjoyment out of the sport.

We have taught golfers of every ability level to learn greater consistency, improve their short games, putting, course management, and to develop a dependable, repeating swing. Golf is amazing in that it requires mastery of fundamentals to produce results. The greatest players concentrate on how they hold the club, how they aim at the target, how they stand and address the ball, and how to do it all in balance. Often I have taught a PGA player one-day, and a beginner the next, and am constantly struck by the fact that each player is working on the exact same fundamentals.

On course instruction is one of the hallmarks of The *Original* Golf School™. Our winter home at the Plantation Inn and Golf Resort includes nine holes of

golf exclusively for Golf School students who really want to hone their game. Other schools try to simulate playing conditions, but we teach our students on a regulation course solely dedicated for the use of our golf school students. By learning "on-course" our students improve not only their shot-making abilities, but also gain valuable course management skills.

We teach year-round, and the winter season is simply too long not to enjoy golf, or to take time to improve your game. That's why The *Original* Golf School™ heads south every winter to the Plantation Inn and Golf Resort in Crystal River, Florida, where the student is surrounded by the wonders of Florida's gulf coast: lofty pines, arching palms, pristine lakes, and quiet estuaries that are home to blue herons, bald eagles, and playful manatees. In the summer we are by the beach at Ocean City, Maryland, or at our home site at Mount Snow, Vermont, where it is possible to be overwhelmed by the lush beauty of the Green Mountains. Each of our school sites possesses its own unique natural characteristics that will inspire and rejuvenate, but I don't want to turn this into a digression on the beauty and scenery around our schools. If you are a school alumnus, you undoubtedly recall spending time outdoors with us.

I hope this book reinforces what you learned during your time with us. If you are ready for a tune-up, or want to refresh what we teach, we welcome alumni with open arms. If you have not attended one of our schools, and would like to learn more, contact us at 800-240-2555, or visit us on the web at www.thegolfschool.com.

> If you think about the game of golf, it is really about hitting a very small ball (about 1 1/2 inches in diameter) into some holes in a much larger ball (about 8,000 miles in diameter).
>
> —Jim Reichert

Golf As A Sport

Golf is an extraordinarily challenging sport. It is enormously rewarding. It's a lifelong sport. Above all else, it is fun! Our objective at The *Original* Golf School™ is to provide students with solid fundamentals that will improve their play and enjoyment of this wonderful game. While the object of golf is to play the course in the fewest possible strokes, I believe the main objective is to have fun.

The charm of the game is that it requires so many varied skills, which gives everyone the opportunity to demonstrate his particular strengths. Power is required for long shots but that power must be tempered with control. Finesse and "feel" are essential to playing delicate shots around the green. Many without power easily score better than their longer-hitting competitors. Playing conditions, and changing weather, also add to the challenge of the sport. How a player adjusts to varying winds, weather, grass and temperature are integral steps in becoming a better player. And, of course, how golfers deal with their emotions while playing also has a great deal to do with their outcome, and their score. The players who remain "cool" through the normal course of the round will best recover from problem situations and maximize their scoring opportunities.

Golf is a wonderful game that anyone can play. Golf is endlessly challenging, and there is no one in the world that feels he has wholly mastered the sport. Go out and play. Come and visit us at The *Original* Golf School™. And most of all, be sure to enjoy yourself!

How To Be A Good Golf Student

It is normal in golf conversation to discuss which professional to seek for help with your golf game. That pro normally gains a reputation for being a "good teacher." In normal golf conversation, however, it is rare to discuss how to become a "good student" and how a player can achieve the most benefit from a professional golf instructor. It is amazing how many "good teachers" are available to golfers at all levels once they make a commitment to being "good students." In his wonderful book, *Five Lessons: The Modern Fundamentals of Golf*, Ben Hogan wrote, "The average golfer is entirely capable of building a repeating swing and breaking 80." Jim and I wholeheartedly believe this, and feel that anyone who is willing to be a good golf student can become a single-digit handicap player.

First, analyze your weaknesses. Golf, as we all know is a multifaceted game that requires the mastery of different skills: from tee shots, to fairway woods, to long irons, to mid irons, to around the green, to mastering putting. The first responsibility "good students" have is to be realistic and to honestly decide what areas of their game are weakest. For instance, if you have a small, manageable, slice on with your woods off the tee but can't get the ball on the green from a greenside bunker, then concentrate your efforts on the bunker shot before working on the slice. A pro would rather help you with an area of your game that is a real problem rather than try to perfect a part of your game that is already quite solid.

To realistically analyze your game, accurately document your last few rounds. See the chart on page 18. Was a particular type of shot frequently played poorly? For instance, missing the green with a short pitch, or badly hooking fairway woods, or perhaps having too many three-putt greens? This is a good time to take pen in hand and actually document your game and record how many strokes you average tee to green. Also keep track of how many putts it takes you to get around the course. Once you have determined your weaknesses, let your pro know. It is the pro's responsibility to help you with your game, but it is your responsibility to tell your pro where your game needs the most help.

GOLF CLUB EQUIPMENT & PLAYING EVALUATION

FITTING SCORE CARD

CIRCLE PAR 3s · SQUARE PAR 5s

CIRCLE WOODS AND IRONS BELOW TO SHOW YOUR SET MAKEUP

Fairways Hit (H) · Missed Left (L) Right (R)
Greens Hit (H) Regulation · Missed Left (L) Right (R) · Short (S) Over (O)
Greenside Bunkers · Hit (H), Out & 1 Putt (1) · Out & 2 Putts (2)
Number of Putts 1, 2, 3, or 4
Total Shots Per Hole

NAME *Steve Gilligan*
COURSE *Moundbuilders C.C.* PAR *72* HDCP *17*
DATE *7-15-86*

WOODS / IRONS

HOLE	W1	2	3	4	5	6	7	I1	2	3	4	5	6	7	8	9	PW	SW	3W	Fairway	Green	Bunker	Putts	Score
1	X		③		X					③	④	⑤		⑦			X			H L R	H L R S O	H 1 2	②3 4	5
②												X					X			H L R	H L R S O	H 1 2	②3 4	4
3	⊗										X								X	H L R	H L R S O	H 1 ②	②3 4	5
④	X		⊗								X						⊠			H L R	H L R S O	H 1 2	②3 4	6
⑤					X														X	H L R	H L R S O	H 1 2	1 ②3 4	5
6	X													X						H L R	H L R S O	H 1 2	②3 4	4
7	⊗											⊗							X	H L R	H L R S O	H 1 ②	②3 4	5
8	X				X										⑧		X			H L R	H L R S O	H 1 2	②3 4	5
9	X											X								H L R	H L R S O	H 1 2	1 ②3 4	5
OUT	7		1		3					0	1	3	1	0	1	1	3		3	3	2 3 4 0 2 0	2 0 2	20	44
10	X												X						X	H L R	H L R S O	H 1 2	②3 4	5
⑪											⊗								X	H L R	H L R S O	H 1 ②	②3 4	4
12	⊗				X												⊠			H L R	H L R S O	H 1 2	1 ②3 4	6
13	X		⊗									X					X			H L R	H L R S O	H 1 2	②3 4	6
14	X																X			H L R	H L R S O	H 1 2	②3 4	4
15	X												X				X			H L R	H L R S O	H 1 2	②3 4	5
⑯															⑧					H L R	H L R S O	H 1 2	②3 4	3
17	⊗				X										⑧					H L R	H L R S O	H 1 2	②3 4	5
18	X		X											⑦						H L R	H L R S O	H 1 2	②3 4	5
IN	7		2		2					0	1	0	1	2	3	0	4		2	5 2 0	4 3 1 1 0	1 0 1	19	43
TOTAL	14		3		5					0	2	3	2	2	4	1	7		5	8 3 2	7 7 1 3 0	3 0 3	39	87

©1985 Ralph Maltby Enterprises, Inc.

INSTRUCTIONS:
- Fill Card Out on Next Tee while Others in Your Group Hit
- Place an "X" in Woods and Irons Section to Indicate Clubs Hit on Each Hole
- Circle any "X" to Indicate any Unsolid Feeling Hit, Regardless of the Result
- Square Any "X" to Indicate a Chip Shot
- Circle Appropriate Letters and/or Numbers in Fairway, Green, Bunker & Putts Column
- At Bottom of "Putts" Column, in the "Total" Block, Write in Total Putts for the Round

COMMENTS: *Work on Putting, Chipping bad today - never chipped close. Pulled most shots - generally unsolid*

This is an example of how a fitting card should be filled out. Please see page 126 for a blank card that you can fill in.

Second, choose your pro. When deciding which golf professional you would like to instruct you, there are three factors to consider:

Credentials. Certified members of the PGA and LPGA are professionally trained in all aspects of the game and are required to keep updated on all new teaching methods.

Track Record. A professional who has instilled confidence in his or her students over an extended period of time usually has the teaching methodology and correction techniques down to a science. It's hard to go wrong with an experienced teacher who has good long-term results.

Personality. Communication is the most important ingredient to achieve positive results in golf instruction. The professional you choose should be a person you can look in the eye and, without feeling uncomfortable, say "I don't understand, could you please explain that again?" The professional/student relationship for the serious player is a long-term one. To be successful, you must feel comfortable.

> **Remember:**
> Good players do not try to hit the ball. They try to create a series of good swings.
> **Golf School Instructor—Peter Platt**

Third, correction by a professional. The very first step in correcting a weakness in a player's game is to analyze the clubs. Quite often a student will have trouble getting the ball in the air off the tee because the driver doesn't have enough loft. Bunker shots can be impossible with a sand wedge that is too heavy. Golf can become a great deal easier with equipment that is professionally fit to your game.

The next step is to make the necessary changes. Swing corrections should not be short-term compensations but should be long-term changes that relate to a clear plan for the type of swing or shot you are trying to accomplish. Relating the changes to that plan is a critical junction for the student as well as the golf pro. This is definitely the time to ask a score of questions if the point or the change is not understood. At the end of each instruction session, the pro should recommend the type of practice you need to facilitate your improvement.

19

Fourth, practice by the student. Nothing delights the true golf professional more than seeing students practice the program which has been recommended for them. With practice, positive results are sure to follow. Making changes requires the ability to think, and those changes are more likely to be accomplished if the student is well rested. Try to hit a few well-thought-out shots with a particular goal in mind. By the end of your practice session, assess how closely you have come to your goal. Do not hit a thousand balls mindlessly on the range. Hitting too many balls will tire your muscles, making them less apt to respond to your new change as well as making it more difficult to concentrate. In fact, you should never hit a ball on the range without having a clear idea of what you want the shot to do.

Without a doubt, intelligent practice that is prescribed by a qualified golf professional is your road to better golf.

Harvey Penick wrote in his *Little Red Book* that when he asks you take an aspirin, you shouldn't take the whole bottle. With your golf swing, just a tiny change can make a huge difference, and the natural inclination is to begin to overdo the tiny change that has brought success. You then exaggerate in an effort to improve even more, and soon you are lost and confused. Remember that just slight adjustments may be all you need.

The Long Game

The ability to hit consistent shots with maximum distance is a product of developing the proper fundamental foundation. There is a progression to this development. The proper grip, alignment and ball position—the position of the ball relative to your stance—will help you develop correct posture. The golf swing is almost impossible to execute correctly and it is highly difficult to develop a repeatable swing unless these elements are in place. Few players, even top PGA pros, ever feel they have truly mastered these fundamentals, so the objective of all golfers should be to create the best possible stance, or "starting position."

The best starting position will allow you to repeat your swing. A starting position that is not sound will require the player to make a variety of compensations in his swing. Having to make "in swing" adjustments will create inconsistent results since you will be making swing alterations in mid-swing. The result is a loss of distance and accuracy.

Mark starts the swing with the triangle formed by his arms and a line across his shoulders.

Mark has established an excellent address position. He has a slight tilt from the hips and his arms are extended, yet relaxed.

TOP LEFT: Notice how his wrists are beginning to hinge. This action is a product of his having a correct grip.

TOP RIGHT: His weight is moving noticeable to his right foot. His body is rotating and starting to coil.

BOTTOM LEFT: The downswing is a natural unloading of the power he has created, and is initiated by a transfer of weight from the back foot to the front foot.

BOTTOM RIGHT: He stays in balance, and his left hip clears just before impact.

Remember:
    Woods don't make contact with the ground.
    Irons make contact with the earth.

Hitting an Intentional Draw: Choke up on club, slightly rotate the club in your hands, close your stance, and play ball back in the stance a bit.

TOP LEFT: His left shoulder and left knee are behind the ball.

TOP RIGHT: He has fully wound up the upper part of his body, and you can sense the power he has created.

BOTTOM LEFT: The swinging action of the clubhead releases the club. Notice how his right forearm crosses over his left forearm.

BOTTOM RIGHT: In the follow through all weight is on the forward foot, the spine is straight, and his body has fully rotated.

- To hit a higher shot, play the ball more forward in your stance.
- To hit a lower shot, play the ball slightly back in your stance.

Hitting an Intentional Fade: Choke up on the club, keep the heel of the club in front of the toe, open the stance, try to make a little outside-in swing.

The Grip

You can't play good golf without a good grip. While discussing the grip may seem boring, it is imperative that it be good. There are many good golfers with bad swings, but no good golfers with bad grips. The golf grip is how we place our hands on the "handle" of the club. The reason the grip is so important and is stressed so strongly by our school staff is because it is the heart and soul of the swing. Your hands will face the target naturally when you swing. If you have the proper grip your hands and the club-face will be square to (face) the target when the club hits the ball. If the grip is not correct you will have to compensate during the swing. Or, you may start to change your alignment to "play for" the incorrect grip. Either way you will not be able to develop a consistent swing. You may compensate for an incorrect grip, or you may over or under compensate for an incorrect grip. You cannot be as consis-tent as you would be if you started with the correct grip.

The standard grip was developed by Harry Vardon, and is popular throughout the world.

To establish the correct grip:

1. Hold the club up so the head of the club is waist high.

2. Square the clubface to the target.

3. Grip the handle with the top hand so it is being held high in the palm and in the fingers. Notice that the pad of your hand and the last three fingers will support the club. This is important, as it will establish the correct amount of wrist action, or hinging, on the backswing.

4. The V formed by the crease between your thumb and forefinger should point toward your back shoulder.

5. To properly place your bottom hand on the club, half close it so a small pocket is formed. Move your hand to the handle and cover the thumb of the top hand, then close your fingers around the handle.

With the top hand we hold the handle so the V formed by the thumb and forefinger point to the back shoulder.

The bottom hand grips the handle a little more in the fingers. Once again the V formed by the thumb and forefinger point to the back shoulder.

6. The V formed by the crease of the thumb and forefinger of your bottom hand should also point to your back shoulder.

Grip pressure should be light. Most golfers hold the club too tightly.

Too much pressure will reduce distance by not allowing proper hinging and will certainly reduce "the feel" you have for the clubhead and clubface, which is essential in all shots. The best barometer is to hold the club firmly enough to maintain control, yet softly enough to feel the clubhead. The club should lie across the top joint of the fingers of the right hand.

You can practice your grip any time of the year. Even 30 minutes a day sitting in front of the television holding the club properly will develop the "muscle memory." You will need to properly hold the club so

that the shaft is pressed up under the pad of the heel of your left hand and lies across the top joint of the forefinger. Pressure should come from the last three fingers and the heel pad. The V should point toward your right eye.

With the right hand, the shaft should lie across the top joint of the fingers, below the palm. The V should point toward your back shoulder.

When both hands are on the club, they should work together. The little finger of the right hand should lock into the groove between the forefinger and big finger of the left, and the left thumb should rest under the right palm.

It is smart to try to pattern your swing after that of a professional player who is close to your size and build. But, only do this if you also imitate his grip. The interlocking grip, with the forefinger of the top hand intertwined between the little finger and ring finger of the bottom hand, is for people who have short fingers, such as Jack Nicklaus. The overlapping grip, with the little finger of the bottom hand wrapped into the hollow between the forefinger and middle finger of the top hand, is the most widely used (Ben Hogan, Sam Snead, Arnold Palmer). The ten-finger, or baseball grip, is good for women and older golfers who may lack strength, and has been good for some professionals (Beth Daniel).

Grip:
1. **Grip clubs properly. Both V's point to your right shoulder.**
2. **Both hands should have equal pressure**
3. **Left arm gets long on backswing and folds on follow through.**

While you work on forming and re-forming your grip, start with the left hand, and hold the club so it runs diagonally from the base of the little finger to the crook of the forefinger. Don't hold the club in the palm. The in-palm position may feel more comfortable at first, but it actually creates tension and reduces mobility of the wrist.

In *Five Modern Lessons*, Ben Hogan says the tips of the thumb and forefinger of the bottom hand should never touch each other. However, some teach that the thumb and forefinger should meld together like a trigger.

Pre-Shot Routine

A pre-shot routine is the series of motions a player makes just prior to initiating the swing. Many golfers easily hit shot after shot on the practice range only to find when they get to the course they do not hit the shots nearly as well. In the practice area we swing freely, but when we get on the course we often begin to feel tension and do not experience the same freedom. The way to carry the feeling of ease from the practice area to the course is by establishing a reliable "pre-shot routine."

We have all noticed these pre shot routine motions by good players. They appear to be nervous gestures or idiosyncrasies. Actually they are part of a set routine to establish consistent results. If a player has the same routine, using the same amount of time, it is likely he will make a repeating swing. Golfers experience pressure, whether it is playing in a club tournament, a major championship tournament, playing with your boss, or even in a game among friends. Normally the greater the pressure the more precise or "careful" you will tend to be. This then translates to spending more time standing over the ball as we go over our mental checklist—sometimes twice. This additional time standing over the ball will certainly increase tension in grip pressure and throughout our body, making a smooth swing less likely.

The concept of a pre-shot routine is to establish a reliable pattern that will give you the best possibility of creating a smooth, repeating swing regardless of the pressure of a given situation.

Each player should establish his own routine. We are all so different in our approach that it would be unrealistic to prescribe an identical routine for every player, but here are some guidelines to help you establish yours:

1. Picture the shot before you hit it. Establish the line of flight by standing behind the ball and drawing an imaginary line from the ball to the target.

2. Pick a line of flight—you may choose to use a piece of grass a few feet in front of the ball, or an object in the background to help you line up.

3. Set the clubface behind the ball and square it to the line of flight.

4. Take your stance. The back foot is first set perpendicular to the line of flight and then the forward foot.

5. Look up at your target (most golfers are comfortable with two or three looks).

6. Make your swing.

> **To tell where you are aimed, take your stance and hold your clubshaft along the front of your thighs. The direction the club is pointing is the direction you are aimed. Laying the club on the ground at your feet is not as accurate.**

As you address the ball and go through your pre-shot routine it is essential to stay in motion. If you stand still over the ball and slowly go over your mental checklist you will get tight, which will restrict motion. All the planning for the stroke should be done before you address the ball. Almost all golfers go through the experience of "self-talk"—the mental checklist of all the swing motions we should or should not do. Self-talk takes time and if it is done while you stand over the ball it will produce tension and reduce motion. The way to produce your best swing is to review the motions you are trying to create, take a practice swing to "feel" the motion, and then try to repeat that feel when you swing through the ball.

The prescription for a pre-shot routine that works may seem long, but it only takes a few seconds. Once you establish a good routine for yourself you will feel a rhythm that will help you play well in all situations.

Your first drive of the day is the most important shot you hit all day. This is true for both professional and recreational players. The tendency is to cut your swing short and forget to shift your weight properly. Take your time. Take a deep breath, or two to relieve tension. Concentrate on having a smooth rhythm during the backswing and accelerate through the shot no faster than you would with a short iron.

Many good players choose to start the swing with a "forward press," which is a slight move with the hands and the right knee toward the target before actually starting the swing. This move will trans-fer some weight to the left foot and then-rock back to the right foot. To make a good backswing you should shift about 60% of your weight to your back foot. This subtle forward-backward move is the easiest way to initiate the weight shift.

The Drive
- **Ball almost in line with left heel.**
- **Square stance**
- **Weight evenly distributed.**
- **Hands even with ball at address.**
- **Align body square to the line of flight.**
- **Grip pressure should be even and relaxed.**

Stance and Posture

I find it helps tremendously to bring a notebook and pencil to the practice tee and to make note of every element of my practice session. I keep track of what I was working on, what adjustments I have made and how it has affected my swing. The next time I go to the practice tee, I simply refer to my notes to see what has been working and what hasn't.

With your stance and posture, the feet should be set about the width of your shoulders, as measured from your heels. Practice this with a five-iron, and lengthen your stance for lower lofted irons and woods, and narrow your stance for shorter irons with more loft. Many golfers take a stance that is too narrow, which I believe hinders their ability to make the proper transition with their weight.

In addressing the ball, your right foot should be at a right angle to the line of flight and the left foot should be turned out about a quarter of a turn to the left, or about 22.5 degrees. To clarify this point, if you placed your left foot so your big toe was pointing directly at the target, this would be a full 90-degree turn from perpendicular to the flight line. So, a quarter turn would be a quarter of the 90 degrees, or about 22.5 degrees. This permits you to transfer weight properly.

A line across your feet should be approximately parallel to the intended line of flight. This is called a "square

32   *Barry's arms are relaxed.*

He tilts from the hips and his spine remains straight.

stance." Some specialty shots will call for an "open" stance. In this stance, a line cross the toes, shoulders, and hips points to the left of the target (for righthanded golfers). This stance is often used to play short shots, particularly out of sand traps. For other specialty shots, use a "closed" stance. In this stance a line across the toes, shoulders, and hips point to the right of the target.

How you stand or address the ball will ultimately determine how you will swing. The stance should be athletic and in balance.

Good posture in golf is achieved by being active, with your weight evenly distributed, and balanced. Anyone can stand straight and then make a baseball-type swing, but one of the challenges in golf is to stand comfortably to the golf ball while it is on the turf and still create a comfortable golf swing. To achieve the proper posture simply tilt from the hips and push your tailbone back to feel balanced. If you only tilt forward, your body weight will move to the front part of your foot. Pushing the tailbone back will move your body weight to the middle of each foot. A good check is to make sure you can wiggle your toes in your shoes. If you are in an athletic position and can do this, chances are you are balanced. If you can't, you're leaning too far forward.

As you get yourself balanced with good posture, your spine will be straight, but at a tilt. In a baseball-type swing the backbone is straight up and down, but in golf the spine is still straight, but tilted. This is what is referred to as "correct spine angle."

Remember to keep your right foot square to the line, and to have the left foot turned out a quarter turn.

The distance you stand from the ball is a result of the tilt you have from the hips and the length of the club. The wedge is the shortest club, so you stand closer to the ball when using it. As you progress to longer clubs, you will stand further from the ball.

Fairway Woods
- **Weight evenly distributed.**
- **Forward ball position and slightly wider stance.**
- **Stand slightly further from the ball.**
- **Hands even with the ball.**
- **Align body square to target.**
- **Check your grip, relax and swing with good tempo.**

The Waggle

The best way to "feel" the shot before you hit it, is to "waggle" the club. Get yourself set and aligned, and address the ball; then "waggle" the club. "Waggles" are short, swing-like actions where the clubhead travels from a position behind the ball to about waist high. The pace of the waggle should match the shot you are about to play. A soft shot, such as a high shot over a bunker should be initiated with a slow, soft waggle. If you are attempting a low shot against the wind, the waggle should be brisk.

You should "stay in motion" while establishing your stance. It should only take a few seconds to make the proper grip, align yourself to the target, take your stance, waggle the club and swing. You should not stand still, or "get stuck" at the address position. Getting stuck will increase tension, limit flexibility and decrease the chance of a smooth swing.

The Waggle is the link between the address and the start of the backswing. As you look at your target and determine what kind of shot you are going to play, you should let your instinct take over and let yourself feel the shot you are about to play. At this stage you should waggle your club back and forth. You should not waggle without a purpose, however. It is important to let the waggle give your mind and body a chance to practice the swing, and you should feel the shot through the waggle. During the waggle the shoulders do not turn, but on the actual swing they do.

Ball position with a middle iron is left center to center.

Ball Position

Unless you are playing a specialty shot, the ball should be played center to forward in your stance. With short irons the ball should be about at the center of the stance. As the clubs get longer, the stance gets wider by moving the back foot. This will place the ball forward in the stance. Simply put, short irons are played from the center of the stance, and longer clubs more toward the forward foot.

How far should you stand from the ball? A lot of players ask that question.

To achieve the correct distance stand straight and hold the club waist high. Allow the upper arms to lightly touch your chest. Now tilt from the hips to reach the ball. The center of the clubface is the exact measure for where the ball should be addressed.

Ball position for a driver is inside the left heel.

intermediary target, square the clubface to the imaginary line, then set your back foot perpendicular to the imaginary line, and then set your forward foot perpendicular to the imaginary line. Your left foot (your forward foot) should be flared out slightly, to allow you to shift your weight. If you draw an imaginary line across your toes, it should be parallel to the initial line of flight.

Alignment

The best swing will only be effective if the clubface is properly aligned to the target. Proper alignment will also foster a better swing because if you are properly aligned, you need make no further compensations. To achieve proper alignment first determine the desired line of flight. The best way to "see" that is to stand behind the ball and draw an imaginary line to the target. If you do this, your perspective will be 100% correct. Next, on that imaginary line, pick a spot a few feet in front of the ball. Once you have this

The Full Swing

You want to develop a solid swing that does not fall apart under duress from competition. A correct swing will, in fact, get better as you put more pressure on it. The good news is that you only need to develop one swing, since you will use the same fundamental swing for every shot you play. For all shots the ball should be played in the same fundamental position, left center in your stance. Your swing will automatically change slightly for each shot. For longer irons

From this angle, notice Sue's excellent posture: arms relaxed; a slight tilt from the hips; her spine is straight.

She begins her backswing by turning the triangle (formed by her arms and a line across her shoulders) away from her target.

At the top of her swing, she has created power by winding up the upper portion of her body.

She begins her down-swing by transferring her weight to the front foot.

36

and woods, your swing will lengthen and it will shorten for more lofted clubs.

When you shorten your swing, for more lofted clubs, it is important that you still shift your weight on the downswing. As you swing, be sure your backswing stays on your normal plane. As your arms approach the level of your hips on the backswing they should be moving parallel with the plane and should stay on a parallel plane throughout the backswing.

At impact her right arm and right hip arrive to the ball at the same time.

The swinging action of the clubhead "releases" the club.

As she releases power, she keeps rotating her body toward the target.

The finish position is relaxed, and all weight is on the front foot.

From a balanced address, swing the club back with the triangle formed by your arms and shoulders. The "center" of your body (the center is the middle of your chest) swings with the club. The left knee is starting to break toward the right knee while the weight of your body moves to the back foot. The wrists begin to "hinge" as a product of a proper grip. At the top of the swing you have created power by "winding up" the big muscles of your upper body. Notice that the "center" is facing directly from your target, and weight has shifted to your back foot.

As you begin the downswing, your weight shifts from your back foot to your front foot. The weight shift initiates the downswing and the hips naturally follow as they release the rest of the body and the legs and arms follow. The shoulders and upper part of the body follow and as your hands release you are supplying the club with tremendous power to launch the ball.

The change of direction from backswing to downswing is a natural un-winding and release of power you have created. The downswing is initiated by this natural unwinding as well as the weight transfer from back foot to front foot.

There are no tricks to solid contact. As you swing the club through the ball and toward the target, the ball merely gets in the way of a good swinging motion. The follow through is the final step of all the prior movements. The "center" has moved toward the target, the club has been fully swung and is held relaxed over the left shoulder, and almost all the weight is on the forward foot.

You rotate your body away from the target on the backswing and then rotate

Perhaps the most common ailment of the recreational golfer is slicing. Just like the common cold, the common slice has numerous causes. However, unlike the common cold the common slice has numerous cures:

1. Don't tighten the grip, relax it.
2. Change your grip, and try a stronger grip by turning both hands equally, bit by bit, to the right.
3. Try using thinner grips because that will promote more wrist action.
4. Try limiting your hip turn on the backswing, so you won't take the club too far inside and then loop over the top.
5. You need to release the club, to square the clubface. Try actually throwing an old club down the range as far as you can. Once the club flies on target consistently, you'll be swinging from the inside with loose arms. This is best done when the range is empty.
6. Strengthen your wrists.
7. Close your stance by pulling your right foot back from the target line. Shift your weight to your left foot on the downswing.

your the body toward the target on the forward swing. The length of your swing is a product of how flexible you are.

Don't be afraid of your long irons. All you need is a little more time to let the swing complete. Don't be in a hurry to start the club down, and make sure you make a complete turn before starting your move from the top of the swing down. When you take the club back too fast, the club starts down out of sequence with your body.

A good drill to use to maintain your spine angle, and to keep you from changing your spine angle during the swing or rotating your chest too early is to put your driver even with your back foot. Put your left hand on top of the shaft. Then, swing your right hand under it, palm down. This will mirror the proper swing.

Long Irons
- Align body square to target.
- Ball position left of center.
- Weight evenly distributed
- Hands even with the ball.
- Check grip, relax and swing with good tempo.

Visualization

Golfers should try to visualize every shot before they try to execute it. The first step in our pre-shot routine should be to visualize the shot. We "see" the shot before it is played, and the image is transmitted to our brain, which tells our muscles what to do. The better we are able to present a clear visual message from the brain to our muscles, the more likely our muscles will execute our vision.

Visualization is particularly important in the short game. In putting, we have to picture the ball rolling, as if it were on rails, toward the hole. This allows the brain to send a message to the muscles about just how hard to hit the putt. In chipping and putting we have to picture the ball landing on the green and then rolling toward the hole. Difficult shots over trouble will become easier if we first visualize them.

Jack Nicklaus writes in *Golf My Way* of the importance he places on visualizing the target and the shot before hitting it:

I never hit a shot, even in practice, without having a very sharp, in-focus picture of it in my head. It's like a color movie. First I "see" the ball where I want it to finish, nice and white and sitting up high on the bright green grass. Then the scene quickly changes and I "see" the ball going there: its path, trajectory, and shape, even its behavior on landing. Then there's a sort of fade-out, and the next scene shows me making the kind of swing that will run the previous images into reality. Only at the end of this short, private, Hollywood spectacular do I select a club and set up the ball.

The Short Game

The first step when chipping or pitching is to visualize how the ball will fly, land on the green, and roll toward the hole. Be sure to account for the break in the green. When chipping you want to get the ball on the ground as soon as possible, so you will be using a middle iron, such as a 5, 6, or 7 if you are just a few feet off the green. You will use an iron with more loft if you are farther from the hole.

When chipping into the wind, select a less lofted club, such as a 5 instead of a 7, so that the wind will not affect the ball as much and the ball will have enough distance to reach the hole. Also be sure to remember that putting surfaces vary in texture and length, so the ball will roll at various speeds. If the green is "fast" you should choose a club with more loft, so the ball will not run by the hole. Distance to the flagstick is also a factor, for instance if you are 6 feet off the green and the pin is fairly close, use a lofted 7 or 8 iron. When the flagstick is on the far side of the green, the better choice would be a 5 or 6 iron. Notice whether you are hitting uphill or downhill, so that you account for the natural speed of the shot.

You can use the same stroke for all of your greenside chips. In actuality it can be an extension of your putting stroke. Keep your wrists very firm and sweep the club through the ball. Don't jab the club into the ground, because you run the risk of stubbing the shot fat. The key is to select the club that will fly the ball a few feet onto the green, then roll it to the hole like it's a putt.

Chip the ball if: the lie is poor; you have a downhill lie; you are feeling stress; the green is hard; or the wind will affect the shot. Pitch the ball if: you have an uphill lie; the lie is good; there is something you must hit over; or if the green is soft.

The best way to improve your short game is to practice. These shots are all about feel, and you should determine what is best for you. Remember the fastest way to shave strokes off your game is to improve your short game. When you have time to practice, don't just bang balls mindlessly on the driving range, but go over to the practice green and work on your short game. A good drill is to take one ball, chip or pitch it toward the hole,

For short chip shots you hold the club (usually a 5, 6, or 7 iron) as you would hold a putter. Stand with your feet close together and position the ball as if you were putting.

then putt it out. Do this over and over, with just one ball. Repeatedly hitting the same shot over and over is not nearly as effective since you can't simulate real play like you can by practicing with one ball.

In an hour practice session, try to spend 40 minutes of that time working on your short game. If you only have a few minutes to warm up before you play, use that time to limber up, and hit some chips and putts. You will begin to feel your touch develop, and you will prepare your muscles for the longer shots.

Pitch Shots

- 9 iron or pitching wedge.
- Open, narrow stance.
- Weight more on left side.
- Ball right center in stance.
- Hands in front of ball.
- No body movement, feet close
- Hit ball crisply.
- To hit over trees, or to get immediate height:
- Play ball more off of left heel.
- Move weight more to right side.

Chip Shots

- 5-6-7 irons.
- Feet close together.
- Square stance.
- Ball in middle of stance.
- No body movement.
- Weight more on left side.
- Hands in front of ball.
- Hit ball in front of green and roll to target.
- For short, greenside chips, use your putting grip.

For the standard pitch shot, use your standard grip and play this shot with a pitching wedge. The feet are fairly close together, arms relaxed and the ball positioned center to right center in the stance.

42

The Flop Shot

This shot is a short, high shot that lands very softly on the green and has little if any roll. Use it when playing over bunkers and hazards. The right club to use is either a sand wedge, or 60 degree wedge. To play the shot: open your stance (aiming your feet, hips and shoulders to the left of the target); position the ball in the center of your stance; and make a big, slow swing. Remember to keep your arms moving through the swing.

For the flop shot, the ball is played slightly forward in the stance.

The tempo for the swing is slow and relaxed.

Grip pressure should be soft.

Allow the loft of the club and the swinging action of the club to lift the ball into the air.

There is some weight transfer.

In the follow through, all weight is forward, and the arms are relaxed

43

Advanced Short Game Techniques

The bladed sand wedge or fairway wood shot. Occasionally the ball will settle down in the grass just off the green, or will roll up against the long grass on the collar of the fringe. The long grass will be between the club face and the ball, and it will be nearly impossible to strike the ball cleanly. If you try to play a standard chip shot in this situation you will probably catch the grass before the ball and only hit it a few feet, or hit the ball too cleanly and skip it across the green. Here you can select a sand wedge, then address the leading edge of the clubface to the equator, or middle of the ball.

The swing itself should be identical to a putting stroke, with a putting stroke grip. The leading edge of the sand wedge will cut right through the grass, hitting the ball at the equator, and the ball will roll like a putt. The same concept can be applied with a fairway wood, which is a shot that seems to have become popular because of the way Tiger Woods has employed it.

The bladed sand wedge is used when the ball is just off the green, up against the collar. It is a fairly advanced shot, but useful to learn.

The long greenside bunker shot. One of the hardest shots in golf is the long bunker shot, of 25 or 30 yards. The standard method is to use a sand wedge, open your stance, and swing through an area behind the ball, taking a full swing. Because the sand acts as a cushion, the ball is usually left well short of the hole, but often players overcorrect and sail the ball over the green.

There are two adjustments you can use to make this challenging shot easier. First, after you take your stance, move about an inch farther away from the ball. This will ensure a shallower swing and will prevent the clubhead from digging too deeply into the sand.

Second, use an iron other than a sand wedge, such as an 8 or 9 iron. Use the same technique as for the standard sand shot: open the stance, and swing through the area behind the ball, removing the cushion of sand and the ball from the bunker. Since the 8 or 9 iron has less loft, the ball will travel farther.

Playing from hardpan. Hardpan is packed ground with little or no grass. If you have a clear line to the pin, you can use a putter. If you need some loft on the shot use a pitching wedge, and play the ball back in your stance, which will create a slightly lower ball flight, but will ensure solid contact.

Occasionally the ball will be behind a bunker, and you will need a high shot that stops quickly. To do this, play it just as you would a standard sand shot: open the stance, swing through an area behind the ball, and follow through.

All three of these methods require some imagination and practice, but can save you several strokes.

Sand Play and Special Situations

Sand bunkers are a strategic part of the game. Some are placed near the green to protect the green and to create challenge for an approach shot, while others are alongside the fairways to challenge accuracy off the tee.

The one area of the golf course recreational players fear most is the sand bunker. While it may appear to take years of practice to master this shot, acceptable results are certainly possible for all golfers.

Learning to properly play out of the sand is a very strategic part of the game. Most players fear the sand so much that they "play away" from sand bunkers at all costs. If there is a sand bunker on the left side of the green, they will aim to the right, even though there may be other hazards there. "Playing away" from bunkers will often add more strokes; and is obviously not the shortest route to the pin.

Sand bunkers are hazards, and the rules state you cannot remove any loose impediments, such as leaves or stones, and you are also not allowed to "ground" the club (touch the club head to the sand) when you address the ball. What you should do is hold the club an inch or two above the sand.

The sand shot (from a good lie) is played from an open stance.

45

As you have an open stance, you will automatically swing the clubhead on a slight outside to inside path.

The tempo should be slow and relaxed.

The downswing begins with a weight shift, as in all golf shots.

Sand Traps
- **Open stance.**
- **Weight evenly distributed.**
- **Hands even with the ball.**
- **Aim 1 to 1 1/2 inches behind the ball, and try to remove a "square" of sand.**
- **Use a normal swing.**

The Proper Club, A Good Sand Wedge

The Sand Wedge was invented in the 1920's by Gene Sarazen, one of the leading players of his time. He, as well as other players, had a great deal of trouble playing from greenside bunkers. The difficulty came from the fact the Niblick (or wedge of that era) would dig into the sand. While taking a flying lesson he had a great idea. He thought he could develop a club that would glide through sand much as the wing of an airplane would glide through the air. Sarazen added weight to the back of the Niblick. This additional metal created a "flange" on the back of the club. The effect was that the club would slide through the sand, throwing a divot of sand, and the ball out of the bunker. His invention, the sand wedge, caught on quickly as Gene Sarazen went on to win the U.S Open, British Open, Masters and P.G.A.

Greenside Bunkers. There are two basic shots from a greenside bunker.
I. If the ball is lying clean and you have a "good lie":
    1. Take a normal grip and posture - Slightly "open" your stance
    2. The ball should be slightly forward in your stance

Allow the loft of the wedge to lift the ball out of the bunker. The sand will act as a cushion for the ball.

A full follow through will ensure that the ball will come out of the bunker.

3. Look at an area behind the ball, about 1 1/2 to 2 inches (this is where the clubhead should enter the sand)

4. Use a normal swing, a swing that would approximate a 3/4 wedge shot (most players do not use enough swing in the greenside bunker). As with all shots, a follow through is important.

The result will be that a divot of sand and the ball will fly out of the bunker. The sand will act as a cushion. Once you have achieved some confidence in playing the ball from the bunker, the next step is to control distance. You control the distance in a greenside bunker by how hard you swing, not by how much sand you take (or how far behind the ball the club enters the sand). For a short sand shot, you use the same technique you would use for a short shot from the grass: choke up a little on the club, feet together, and use a short swing. As the distance increases, you use a longer and fuller swing. The length of the follow through is a good way to gauge the distance of the sand shot.

A ball lying cleanly in a bunker.

47

A ball in a depression in a bunker.

How to Play in Different Types of Sand.

The texture of sand will vary from courses in the North to those in the South. Sometimes, the texture of the sand may vary from one course to another. Getting a "feel" for the sand of a given course is the reason we see PGA and LPGA tour stars practicing at a tournament site. They are not trying to perfect their technique; they are trying to acquire feel.

The general rule is: the softer the sand, the softer the ball will come out of the sand bunker. If the sand is firm, the ball will "jump" out quickly. If the sand is very soft, use a long full swing. If the sand is firm, use a less full swing. You use the length and fullness of the swing to accomodate different situations.

Gaining confidence in the bunker is a product of knowledge and practice. A good way to practice to gain that confidence is to aim well behind the ball and swing hard. You'll be surprised how softly the ball comes out of the bunker.

II. If the ball is not lying cleanly, but is in a footprint, a depression or in the mark made when it entered the bunker. To play this "buried" lie:

1. Take a normal grip and posture

2. The ball should be addressed well back in the stance

3. Look at an area behind the ball, about 1 inch

4. Now swing the clubhead down into the sand directly behind the ball.

Because you play the ball "back" in your stance for this shot, the clubhead will stay in the sand. A follow through is not really possible. The loft of the club-head and the downward pressure of the club will "pop" the ball up out of the lie.

This is a difficult shot for you to control distance. The ball will come out of the bunker with little or no backspin and will "run" quite a bit.

Fairway Bunkers. Fairway bunkers are those sand bunkers that are alongside the fairway, leaving a lot of distance to the green. There are two parts of the fairway bunker shot: the plan and the execution.

The plan should be one that exercises good course management. If you misplay this shot, you may wind up under the "lip" of the bunker, on the way to a high score on the hole.

First, assess what club will easily loft the ball out of the lie and over the front of the bunker. You may think a 5 iron will just clear the lip. If so, you should choose

A Greenside bunker shot.

a 6 or even a 7 iron to play the shot. By always selecting a more lofted club, you will insure you have enough loft to get out of the bunker and; turn a difficult shot into a fairly easy one. Added confidence from knowing you have the percentages in your favor will help you make a freer, more confident swing.

Second, in the execution of the fairway bunker shot, you attempt to hit the ball as "cleanly" as possible. If the clubhead hits the sand before the ball, the "cushion" effect we try to achieve in the greenside bunker shot occurs and you lose distance. There are 3 steps to take to hit the ball cleanly:

1. Choke up on the club, a shorter club will be less likely to hit the sand behind the ball.

2. Move the ball "back" a little in the stance and (for my advanced players) actually try to hit the middle of the ball with the bottom portion of the club.

The most common errors when playing out of sand are: standing flat-footed and decelerating due to fear of hitting over the green.

It was suspected the great Gene Sarazen found it so easy to play out of bunkers that when he was competing in tournaments he would intentionally hit into them, just to give the crowd the thrill of watching him hit out. The reality is that the bunker shot is one of the easiest in golf, but most beginners are terrified at the idea of having to play out. The bunker shot allows for a tremendous margin of error. In fact you don't even have to hit the ball on a short bunker shot, because you are blasting the sand behind the ball.

The fairway bunker shot.

Putting

Depending upon your level of play, the number of putts you hit per round is between 1/3 to 1/2 of the total amount of strokes you will execute for the entire round. Improving this aspect of your game is the fastest way to shave strokes from your score and lower your handicap.

The putting grip is different from the grip we use in full shots. In the putting grip the handle is held more in the palms as we do not want the hinging that is required in the full swing. Place both hands on the handle so the thumbs are on top of the handle and you can feel the handle in the lifeline of both hands.

Many top players and low handicappers favor a reverse overlap grip. To use this grip, slide the forefinger of the top hand down and cover the fingers of the bottom hand. This helps both hands work together.

The putting stroke is a pendulum-type action.

For this stroke, use your arms, and shoulders, with a minimum of wrist action.

Hold the putter handle in the left palm.

Then the right palm.

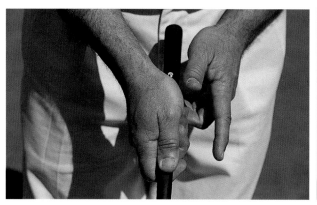

Slide the left forefinger down alongside the fingers of the right hand.

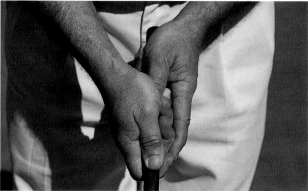

Both hands are now working together, facing the target.

There are many variations on the putting grip. An excellent option is to cross your hands and put the left hand low, for right handed players. It's best to try a few options to see which grip feels best. You want to avoid having any wrist or hinge action, so the palms of each hand should face each other, staying square to the clubface. This lack of hand action will produce a pendulum-type stroke, and you will feel as if you are moving your arms and shoulders together. The size of the stroke should match the length of the putt. Matching the size of the stroke to distance is a product of practice. Always strive to keep the tempo even.

Reading Greens.

Start to read the green by looking at the overall position of the green as you approach it. As you get closer, you can begin to get a feel for the portion of the green where the hole is and how your ball will roll toward it. You can visualize the slope and contour of the green by imagining how water would flow on it. It also helps your perspective to see the green from several different angles.

54

Remember:
1. Putting distance determines the length of the backswing.
2. Stroke with your shoulders and upper arms.
3. Follow through on putts and don't decelerate.
4. Using a "Reverse Overlap" grip straightens the tendons in the back of your left hand and makes your hands work more as a unit.

Putting Aids:
- Always try to hit the ball far enough.
- Keep blade square to the target.
- Do not move your head.
- The palms of your hands goes directly toward target.
- Keep your head directly over ball.

Putt with your eyes shut:

Your sense of feel for all of your golf strokes can be increased by closing your eyes. With all of your focus on the movement your body, the sensations become more clear and your touch and feel improve. This exercise will help increase the feel with any club, however only with putting could this be practically used when hitting the ball. After some practice, you will find your sense of feel is increasing, and you may be surprisingly accurate. You will learn to hit the ball squarely without looking at it. Putting blindly will help you increase feel and trust, and will help you more fully trust looking at the hole while putting.

Understanding "The Lie"

Identifying "The Lie" (how the ball sits in the grass) is actually the first step in managing your game. Sound contact is achieved when the middle of the club-face can cleanly strike the middle of the golf ball. There are many instances when it may be difficult to match the center of the clubface to the center of the golf ball. Examples would be if the ball were lying in a depression or deep in the grass. It takes a lot of experience to identify the lie. Following are a few guidelines to understanding lies:

Deep Grass. When the ball sits in deep grass, the challenge to the player is to get sufficient loft to get the ball in the air and still achieve distance. Deep grass will actually turn the clubface during the swing, thereby reducing the effective loft. The best solution to play well out of deep grass is to choose a club with extra loft. The 7 iron will actually travel a 6-iron distance when played from long grass. Allow the loft of the club to lift the ball out of the rough.

Ball in a depression. This shot is hard, as it appears, because it is difficult to get the ball airborne. As in playing the ball out of deep grass, choose a club with extra loft. You always want to try to turn a difficult shot into an easy shot. When playing out of a depression:

1. Choose an easy club to hit, one with extra loft, and

2. Play the ball back a little in your stance. A good general rule when assessing your lie is to check if the middle of the clubface can easily meet the middle of the golf ball. If not, choose a club with extra loft, one that is easy to hit.

Downhill Lie
- Ball played toward back foot.
- Hands even with ball.
- Check grip and swing smoothly.

Sidehill Lie
If ball is lower than the level of your feet:
- Aim slightly to the left of your target.
- Use one club longer.
- Ball played in center of stance.
- Weight evenly distributed.

If ball is higher than level of your feet:
- Aim slightly to the right of your target.
- Weight is evenly distributed.
- Ball played about center of stance.
- Check grip and swing smoothly in both instances.

If you have a downhill lie, play the ball back in your stance.

Equipment:

A Brief History And The Case For Custom Clubs

Holding a modern golf club links you to a 600-year-old legacy. Recorded in the parliamentary statute books of Scotland in the 1400's, golf was once banned because it interfered with archery practice. Golf can be traced to the mid-1800's when Allen Robinson became the Champion of Scotland. He was Keeper of the Greens, the first professional, and a third-generation ball maker; the ball of the day being a Feathery, a leather pouch stuffed with feathers.

His assistant, Tom Morris, was playing St. Andrews one wet morning and ran out of balls because they were all water logged. He borrowed a ball made from gutta percha, a new innovation that was solid and impervious to moisture. Word spread that Morris was playing a Guttie. By the time he reached the 18th hole, Robinson was waiting for him and a bitter altercation took place because Morris, by playing the new ball, had basically endorsed the Guttie over Robinson's Feathery.

That altercation over the new solid ball escalated golf ball and club development. The soft Feathery demanded a long slashing swing with club heads made from local hard woods. The more durable Guttie allowed harder shots, so irons were developed to overcome hazards and difficult lies. Mashie Nibliks for sand and deep grass, small Rut irons to get out of cart tracks and larger Track irons to recover from large indentations made by horses' hooves.

Shafts were made from native woods, with ash predominating until hickory was imported from America. Hickory was the choice for 70 years, and since shafts came from different trees, care was needed to get matching shafts. Shafts were hand-shaved and sanded to achieve "spring" for each player. The feel of a club was so personal that players could identify theirs blindfolded.

In 1894 a black smith developed a solid spring steel shaft, but it wasn't until 1911 when a drawn steel shaft offered better performance than hickory. Steel shaft acceptance came with Billy Burke's win in the 1931 US Open at Inverness

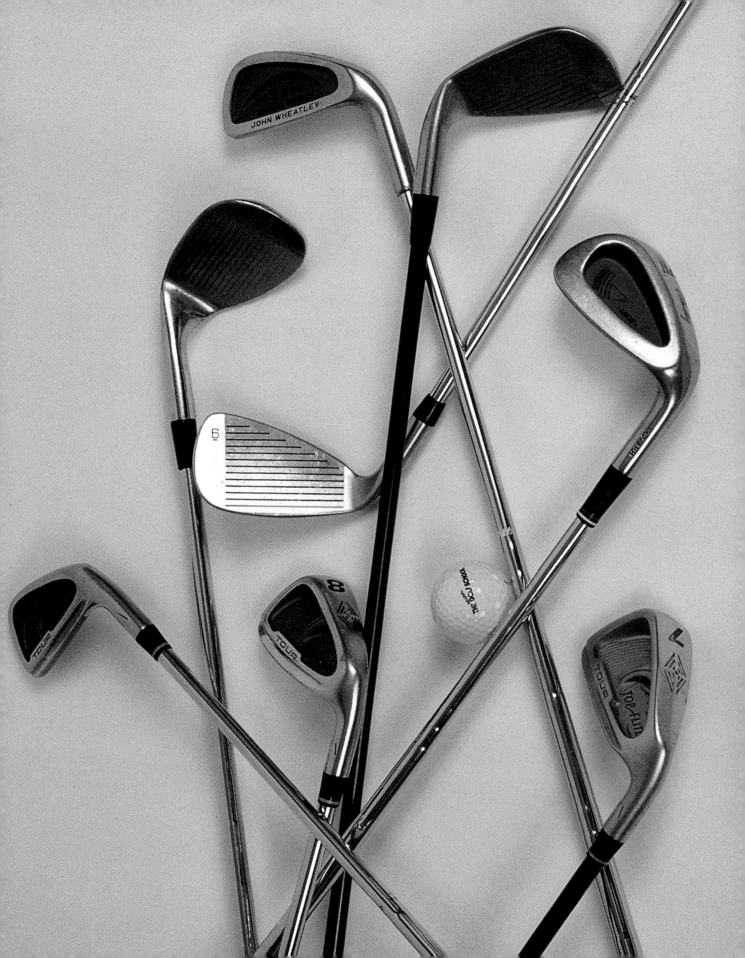

Country Club. Johnny Fischer's 1936 US Amateur win was the last major championship for hickory shafts. Johnny Farrel's U.S. Open win in 1928 with a cast aluminum driver was the first major won with a "metal wood".

As shaft technology expanded, so did the quality of club making. Shaft flex became more precise and methods of measuring flex were developed. The basic equipment of the day was a deflection board—a shaft or fully assembled club would be attached in a clamp, then a weight, normally six pounds, would be hung on the tip end. The amount of bend was a guide to the shaft flex, and the shape of the bend was important to the shaft designers as they studied the variations of curve in relation to weight and balance. Robert Adams of Waban, MA, invented a swing weight scale in the early 1920's. Alistair Cockran suggested in his book, *The Search For The Perfect Swing*, that shaft flex be tested by frequency, which inspired Dr. Brailey to develop his shaft system.

Kenneth Smith, a notable club maker was the first to notice the importance of balance in producing matched sets of clubs. Producing sets that matched flex and balance was an important advancement, and enabled club makers to produce clubs that were preferable to hickory in the early 1930's.

Twenty-seven years after Billy Burke won the 1931 U.S. Open with steel shafts, Dick Mayer won the same championship on the same course with fiberglass. Fiberglass quickly replaced aluminum, but then lost favor to light steel in the late 1960's. Graphite shafts were introduced in the 1970s but couldn't meet all standards generally expected from high quality steel. Recently, innovations in adhesives and assembly procedures made graphite competitive.

The evolution of the handle is interesting. The first grips were thin strips of leather wound around a wooden shaft. Eventually tar was applied to the shaft and then strips of wool were wrapped around the shaft to build up the diameter. Old blankets worked well as they dampened the sting from a miss-hit shot. Soft sheep skin leather wrapped over the blanket gave a comfortable grip. This application method lasted for about one hundred years.

As club heads and shafts evolved, so did the handle. The grip end of steel shafts was a shade smaller than hickory. Players began demanding a larger grip size in the left hand, which was solved by winding crepe paper around the butt end of the shaft to the newly required size and then tapering the diameter gradually to meet the shaft. In 1947 Thomas Farwick was looking for a material for his Airflex Clutch. When visiting a developmental service laboratory in Akron, Ohio, he saw a test run on the manufacture of condoms. Being an avid golfer he thought a grip for a golf club could be made from latex and rolled onto the grip end of a club. The beginning of the slip-on grips wasn't easy, but the Farwick Flex-Grip was born. There was resistance to the new grip because of the use of rubber cement as an adhesive, which was messy to use and unpleasant to inhale. Jim Karns solved the problem when he bought a shirt and noticed two-sided tape was used to hold the collar in place. The tape was adopted and wound around the butt end of the shaft, then coated with activator that allowed the grip to be slipped into position; eventually replacing rubber cement.

By 1956, Victor East, working with Jim Karns, introduced the all-weather Golf Pride Victory Grip, by adding woven cotton thread into the rubber compound. By 1966 the Victory Grip was still the choice of the P.G.A., and still is.

Today, there are clubs matched to frequency, swing weight and balance. The late 20th century golf boom is due to the development of offset irons with peripheral weighting, which offers beginners a better chance of hitting the ball. Shafts are better, offsets work against slicing, and peripheral weighting gets the ball in the air. Earlier stiff wooden shafts, with thin straight blades contributed to a slice, and many left golf in frustration between 1900 and 1965. If you were not a natural, it was difficult to play as equipment only suited the best players.

Today's high handicappers should play with offset irons unless they have visual problems with alignment. If the straighter hosels assist alignment, remember that a softer shaft may be needed to help overcome the possibility of slicing. All iron soles must have sufficient bounce. Straight, sharp leading edges should be avoided, as they tend to dig or snag on undulating fairways.

There are horses for courses, and one iron head will not satisfy all players. The teacher and club maker should guide the player toward clubs that are best suited for his game. Good players playing with offsets with stiff shafts cannot play for long periods without experiencing fatigue or injury as they are working against a hooking club and subconsciously compensating. This compensation will show up as a back problem, an elbow problem or some sort of wrist problem.

The question often asked is, "With the ever increasing improvements in club manufacturing, why the need for custom clubs?" Some people play with correct mass-produced clubs, but not everyone fits the average size, strength, and shaft flex that comes from a large manufacturer.

The club should maximize the energy potential and performance of a golf swing. Use a club with a shaft too stiff and you can expect one or more of the following: a thin shot with a shallow divot; a lower flight; less distance; tennis elbow; or a hitting action that causes the right hand to get strong under the shaft. A shaft too soft produces a deep divot; sprayed shots or a high fade. A grip too large tends to produce a fade. A thin grip decreases power since the club may spin in the fingers and produce a tendency to draw the ball. A lie angle too upright with the correct shaft produces a divot too deep in the toe with a sliding fade, and a lie angle too flat produces a divot too deep in the heel with a hooking flight. A correctly-fitted club will compliment the swing, but a club—no matter how well it is fitted—cannot correct a swing flaw. A club fitter will understand this and have the integrity to explain when the club fits and when the swing needs a correction.

Twenty years ago, clubs were considered fitted, if the loft and lies were checked at the point of purchase, and all the shafts were the correct length and swing weight. With the introduction of

frequency matching, a better fitting system had emerged. Four systems of frequency slopes were patented but only one slope angle worked for all levels of ability. Even when the club maker builds a set of clubs on the correct slope, it is no guarantee of perfect performance unless he has a thorough understanding of shaft balance. When everything is correct the shaft will load at the top of the swing and unload perfectly at impact.

A club maker must have a thorough understanding of: head designs and performances, the characteristics of shaft design and performance, and have the experience necessary to select the correct combination of both to maximize performance. There is more to it than just shaving the shaft for a little more whip, but club makers of all eras faced the same problems and solved them with the available experience and technology.

The next time you handle your clubs you should enjoy knowing your 600-year link with the past, and you should remember to play in the same tradition of those founding players from Scotland: play the ball as it lies, play the course as you find it and leave it better than you found it.

The Three Most Important Clubs

Herbert Warren Wind wrote that the three most important clubs were, in order: the putter, driver and wedge. He said he had asked Ben Hogan, who said THE three were, in order: the driver, putter and wedge.

Wind reasoned that you hit the driver 14 times a round, but during the same round would have 23-25 putts that are outside the "gimmie" range, but that you could make. A 5-foot putt counts one stroke, the same as a 290 yard drive, but the putt may be more significant to your score. Good driving can give you a good psychological boost, but nothing is more psychologically reassuring than sinking putts. Your confidence will soar, and your opponent will feel deflated.

Club Selection And Fit

	Loft	Beginner	Average Golfer	Good Golfer
Approximate Yardage From Clubs				
Driver	10 degrees	190	220	250
3 Metal	15	170	210	225
5 Metal	21	150	195	205
2 Iron	18	145	180	190
3 Iron	22	135	170	180
4 Iron	26	125	160	170
5 Iron	30	120	155	165
6 Iron	34	115	145	160
7 Iron	38	105	140	150
8 Iron	42	95	130	140
9 Iron	46	80	115	125
Wedge	52	70	100	110
Sand Wedge	56	55	80	95

Course Management

We practice to develop the many parts of the game: putting, short game, long game. The score we post is not only a measure of how proficient we have become in these areas but also how well we manage each shot. Golf is like chess in the sense·that you have to plan your next move. If you can't reach the green with your next shot you may choose to stay well short of the green in order to ensure a full shot into it.

Understanding that golf is like chess by planning your first stroke (move) with the idea of making the next stroke (move) as easy as possible. The classic example of this is when you are playing short of a hazard and hitting the ball in position for an approach to the green. You should play the lay-up shot to a part of the fairway that is level and at a distance from the green from which you are confident. You have a much better chance of success if you have an 80-yard approach shot from the fairway than a 30-yard approach from the deep rough.

Use good course management to get the percentages in your favor by playing smart shots and not taking unnecessary chances. For instance, you have driven the ball 200 yards off the tee and into the right rough on a 420-yard hole. The ball is nestled down in the grass, and if you try to hit a fairway wood out of the lie, which you are probably not likely to do successfully, you will probably still

be 40 yards short of the green. If you use a 7 iron for the same shot, at which you will probably be successful, you will be 80 yards short of the green. In both cases you will have a relatively short wedge to the green, but the difference in accuracy between a 40-yard and an 80-yard shot for your third stroke is minimal. By using the 7 iron instead of the fairway wood you have put the percentages for success in your favor. Never take a chance if it won't save a stroke.

While there are countless examples of good course management, following are a few guidelines that should help you save strokes:

Off the tee—Getting the ball in play is the objective. If you are having trouble with your driver, use a #3 metal wood to make sure you hit the ball in the fairway. Don't make the mistake of trying to gain distance at the expense of accuracy.

Approaching shot to the green—Use enough club. Choose a club for this shot that will easily reach the middle of the green. Many players try to use a club that they have to hit 100 percent perfect to reach the green. The target on most approach shots should be the center of the green, not the flagstick. Aiming at the center of the green rather than the flagstick will give you a much greater margin of error.

Long Grass—The first objective is to get the ball up and out of the lie. Choose a club with plenty of loft even if that means you may not able to reach the green.

Trust your swing; don't try to overpower this shot, but allow the loft of the club and the force of your swing to fly the ball up and out of the lie.

Putting—There are two basic approaches:

Long putts—The objective here is to "lag" the ball close enough to the hole to give you a good shot at two-putting the green. Analyze the amount of "break" first, and then put most of your concentration on distance. Take a few practice strokes and try to match the length and size of your putting stroke to the distance you are trying to hit the ball.

Short putts—These should be played aggressively, and you should always hit a short putt with enough speed to at least go past the hole by one foot. Having enough speed minimizes the "break", reduces the influence of some imperfections on the green, and most importantly, guarantees you will reach the hole. We have all fallen in love with the line on a short putt and left the putt short. That is one of the most frustrating ways to waste a stroke.

Some good general course management rules are:

Think ahead—where do you want to play your next shot.

Always play the shot you **know** you can hit. You should choose the club and attempt the shot you are most comfortable with. Attempting the high-risk shot puts doubt in your mind, increases tension, and makes a successful shot very unlikely.

Eight Ways To Lower Your Score:

1. *Practice:* There is no substitute for hard work on the putting green, around the green, and on the range.

2. *Use Enough Loft:* Many beginning golfers don't use a club with enough loft and they become frustrated because they find themselves unable to get the ball in the air. A consequence of this is that they try to overcompensate on their next shot.

3. *If You Can't Get A Clean Shot, Play It Safe:* Rather than take several shots to get out of a bad lie, take an unplayable lie penalty. It will only cost you one stroke, and maybe save you several.

4. *Think:* Don't try to execute the 1 in 100 shot. Be conservative if you are facing an uncertain decision. For instance, use a 3 metal instead of a driver if you are erratic off the tee.

5. *Learn to get out of the sand:* The shot really is not as intimidating as it seems

6. *Don't doubt yourself:* Don't psyche yourself out by thinking about Out-of-Bounds, water, sand, etc. Focus on the target area, and don't let the hazards dominate your thoughts.

7. *Shoot for the fat part of the green:* If the flagstick is in a tough position, just work to get the ball on the green. Don't get taken by a "sucker" pin placement unless your game is really working.

8. *Let your clubs work for you:* Trust your swing and let your equipment do the job for you.

Problems:

Slicing, Hooking, Pulling, Shanking, Skying, Scuffs, and Topping are all caused by not sticking to the fundamentals.

Solutions:

If you experience any of these, always check to make sure your:
Grip is correct, with your hands in front of the ball.
Weight is shifting correctly, and that you are not swaying.
Stance is athletic and you are slightly flexing your knees.
Arms and hands follow through.
Swing is smooth, and in rhythm.
Stance is not too far from the ball, or you are reaching for the ball.

Be sure you are not fearing the shot, regardless of the situation, pressure, or who is watching. Take a deep breath, relax, rid yourself of tension, and swing with good speed, tempo and rhythm. Never rush your shot, life is too short.

Weather:

- If wind is behind, play the ball slightly more forward than normal.
- If wind is in your face, close the club slightly, and play the ball further back than normal, and take 1 or 2 more clubs longer than normal.
- In crosswinds, use a less lofted club than usual. Hit your shot toward the side that the wind is blowing from to correct for influence from the wind.

Fairway Bunkers:

If the ball is lying clean, hit with the same club, plus one, you would use in fairway. You must hit the ball first, not sand. Hit below the centerline of the ball. On bad lies, use any club that will get you in the fairway.

Wet Ground:

Always hit the ball first, not turf. Try to hit just below center of ball.

High Grass:

Again hit the ball below the center line, before turf.

In Rough:

Check for a secure grip. Do not over-strain and "muscle" the grip. A good firm grip will eliminate club twisting, etc.

Course and Hole Ratings

Even though par for a course may be 72, it will not necessarily have a high rating. A standardized system is in place so courses can be compared to one another. This is to ensure that a golfer's handicap reflects his overall golfing ability rather than simply how well he plays a particular course.

Factors that are considered include: the overall length, the altitude at which the course is situated, the size of fairway target areas, difficulties near the target areas, size and location of green, and slope of the ground.

Individual holes are also rated using the above factors, and are then listed from 1 to 18, with 1 being the most difficult and 18 the easiest. This is called the stroke index and it is important when determining whether a player receives a shot on a hole according to his handicap.

75

The Mental Game

Jim and I could not write a golf instructional book without some discussion of the mental aspects of the game, a topic that is relatively neglected. This is the game that is played in the mind of the player, and is played against obstacles such as self-doubt, nervousness, lapses in concentration, and wherever the habits of the mind interfere with excellence in performance. This is where the unconscious mind needs to get the conscious mind out of the way so the player can execute without being overly concerned with mechanics.

The instances where the mind inhibits results include:

1. Whenever you get into a pressure situation. For instance, you have to make a short pressure putt, and as you stand over the ball you feel yourself getting nervous and tense.

2. You know you're doing something wrong, but just can't seem to break the bad habit.

3. When you practice, you play great, but as soon as you get onto the course you fall apart.

4. When you really try hard and really concentrate to execute the stroke perfectly, you MISS the shot. But, sometimes you can just spontaneously walk up to the ball, and without even thinking perfectly nail the shot.

5. You'll take several practice swings, and try hard to remember exactly what to do right. The practice swings feel great, and you are very focused on making the necessary corrections, however, when you actually make the shot you experience mental lapses right in the middle of the swing. You are then astonished that you didn't remember to make the correction you had just been focusing on only seconds earlier, and indeed forgot about in mid-swing.

During the typical lesson, as the pro is working with the student, the pro will point out several adjustments the student needs to make. These adjustments should make the student more technically proficient, but once the student gets out on the course he must let his instincts take over. Jim told me of teaching his father-in-law how to blast out of a trap. His father-in-law was a decent golfer, about a 16 handicap, but had never mastered the shot.

positioned the ball properly, took the club back nicely, and absolutely fluffed the shot because he swung too softly. Jim said, "You swung too softly." His father-in-law said, "Oh, yeah, I did. I guess I forgot to swing hard." The one element of the stroke he had tried to remember was the one thing he didn't do. Everything else was absorbed and reproduced without any instruction or discussion. The point here is that sometimes images are better than words, and too much instruction can be worse than none.

When you finish your round, look at your "potential" score, in addition to looking at your actual score you happened to make. This will breed confidence and will show you what you are capable of. This will also help you be objective in looking at your weaknesses. Analyzing your worst-hole scores gives you an idea of where to make improvements.

Jim decided he would skip a discussion of grip, stance, ball placement, and swing paths, and instead asked his father-in-law to just watch him hit several shots. Jim wanted him to get a visual image of how the shot should be played, and his father-in-law was to repeat the image in his mind several times, then let his body imitate the swing.

After Jim had hit five shots, his father-in-law imagined doing the same, and said to Jim, "I noticed that you really swing hard at the ball. I always try to scoop out the ball by swinging softly." Jim didn't reply, and instead asked him to try the shot and let his body imitate the shot. His father-in-law took the correct stance,

Think about when you hear players being interviewed after a fabulous performance. Oftentimes they will say, "I was in the zone," or, "I was playing out of my mind," or "I was totally unconscious." Many athletes know that in order to achieve a peak performance they cannot be concerned with thinking about mechanics. The athlete who is a peak performer is not playing without consciousness, and in fact is keenly aware of the course, the ball, the elements, and perhaps his opponent, but he is not aware of giving himself a lot of instructions, or corrections to his swing. He is thinking about the game but is comfortable with his mechanics. The player gets immersed in the flow of the game, but does not have to try too hard to execute. Usually the flow ends when the player begins to concentrate too hard on his mechanics.

Jim told me of an instance a few years

and proceeded to shoot an even-par 72. His swing had an even tempo, his putting was sharp, and he played beautifully. Two days later he went out again, this time to play Osprey Point, a much, much easier course. He was really determined. He was going to break par. After all, he played so well on the much tougher Ocean Course. He was focused. He was tuned in. He was lucky to break 90 with an 89. His swing was erratic, his tempo was off, and he missed five three-foot putts. He was over-trying. He was trying to exercise control, but as soon as he did that he lost control, whereas two days earlier his mind was relaxed and he let his body execute without interference.

So, how can you learn to "play out of your mind" on purpose? The goal here is to function without interference from thoughts, and to be in a state of concentration where the mind lets the body into the game and the mind does not interfere. As humans, we have a tendency to interfere with our own ability to perform, and it is because of this self-interference that we are only able to perform at our highest levels for brief periods of time. In order to "play out of our minds," we have to get out of our own way.

Tim Gallwey writes about this eloquently in his 1974 book *The Inner Game of Tennis*, and then extrapolated his thoughts in 1979 to *The Inner Game of Golf*. His thesis was that in order for the golfer to have control over his body, he must first gain control over his mind. He believes that the less a golfer tries the more fluid his swing will be and the easier it is to achieve the optimum coordination and timing that produces the true golf swing. He also believes that

ago when he was in Kiawah Island on a family vacation. He had not played for six months, and the first day there played The Ocean Course, the site of the 1991 Ryder Cup. He was running late, and didn't even have time to hit balls on the range. He got to the first hole, limbered up a little, took a few practice swings,

conscious instruction interferes with unconscious execution. Consider for a moment the acts of brushing your teeth, tying your shoes, or turning on a light switch. Think about any of these actions and try to come up with written instructions to perform each. Then try to execute each of these by following your instructions. It's not easy if you describe the action in detail because your mind is so occupied with following the mechanics.

The goal is to not be caught up in the mechanics so your alertness can be heightened and your actions can seem excellent and simple. Your actions seem to flow effortlessly, and your golf shots are made as if they were the easiest imaginable. It's at these moments you wonder what you ever thought was difficult about the game because your mind is relaxed and quiet, and your body is free of tension. This is because you have control over your concentration and your attention. A terrific byproduct is that the more you master "relaxed concentration" in golf, the more you can raise the quality of your performance in any activity. Relaxed concentration cannot be forced. If you think you must concentrate to make a good shot, you will probably force it. The key is to let your mind relax and your awareness of feel will pick up.

Still, the most important fundamental in golf is neither grip, stance, swing, nor relaxed concentration. The most important fundamental is to know why you play the game. You are playing to be outside with friends, breathing fresh air, getting exercise, and testing yourself against the course. While the number of strokes you take stays on the scorecard, what you learn stays with you and can be used to benefit your life.

Playing In The Wind

Wind is the most significant weather factor we have to consider, especially as it pertains to club selection. Wind is fascinating in that it is the most powerful natural force that is invisible. The ability to control the flight of the ball, high or low, is a skill that will greatly help every golfer to post a better score. It's good to remember the old adage "when it's breezy, swing easy." Swinging easily will help you remember your balance and avoid trying to overpower the wind; both keys to making solid contact and maintaining control.

Hitting the ball high. You may want to "ride the wind" if the wind is coming from behind you. To hit the ball high, use a higher lofted club than you normally would; play the ball a little more forward in your stance and swing to a full follow through.

Hitting the ball low. This is a key skill to acquire because you usually want to keep the ball low against the wind and often you hope to keep the ball low irrespective of the direction the wind is blowing. To hit the ball low, choose a less lofted club, position the ball slightly back in your stance (to the right of center if you are right-handed), choke up on the club an inch, and swing smoothly with a low follow through.

When playing in a crosswind, you should try to visualize how much influence the wind will have on the flight of the ball. If there is a strong left to right wind on an approach shot, you should pick out a target that is well left of the flagstick. The force of the wind and your normal ball flight determine the amount of influence the wind will have on your

To keep the ball low, use a club with less loft; for instance a 6 iron instead of a 7 iron.

Choke up on the handle of the club about 1 inch.

Position the ball back in the stance.

Remember to "Swing easy, when it's breezy."

Keep the swing smooth.

A low follow-through will help keep the ball low against the wind.

If you normally hit a left to right shot you will need to allow for a little more wind influence. It's always a good idea to use the wind and not overpower it. If you try to overpower the wind you normally will force a high ball flight and lose control.

What may seem like a light breeze where you are standing may actually turn out to be a fierce gale along the intended flight of your ball. Before you play your shot, you can check the wind with any of the following:

Flag: A fluttering flag on the green is a crucial indicator of how the wind is blowing, and how it can affect your shot.

Water: Check the ripples on any surrounding body of water.

Tree tops: Look at the highest branches of trees along the intended line of flight of your ball.

Grass test: Take a small handful of grass and throw it in front of you, and notice how it falls.

Golf Myths

There is no shortage of advice in the game of golf. Well meaning friends often offer suggestions about he game that not only do not help you improve, but actually inhibit improvement. These are the main "Myths of Golf":

Keep Your Head Down: This is undoubtedly the most often given piece of advice the recreational player hears. When you hear this, your instinct is to bury your head against your chest, which ruins your posture. Establishing and maintaining good posture will allow for a free-swinging motion.

Keep The Left Arm Straight: The golf swing should be free flowing, and trying to keep your left arm straight will increase tension and reduce motion. The left arm will be long on the backswing, just as the right will be long, or extended, on the follow through, but at no time is either arm stiff.

Pull Down With the Left Arm: Both hands swing the club. There really is no pulling or pushing because the hands work together.

Keep Your Head Perfectly Still: This will restrict motion. Your head should move a little during the swing as you transfer your weight back and then through the swing.

The Don'ts: Very often well-meaning friends will tell you what to do or what not to do just as you are about to swing, or as you are preparing to swing. Remember that the ultimate "don't" is no motion at all. The fear of doing something wrong will increase tension and decrease motion. In order to improve your game, you should learn what to do by understanding what is right for your swing. The only way to overcome these misconceptions is to learn the fundamentals, stick to them, concentrate, practice and listen to your pro. Try not to listen to tips from your brother-in-law, after all you don't listen to him when he gives you tips on the stock market.

Conditioning

There are few competitive sports today where the participants do not physically train for competition. Training is a must if you expect to perform at your best. However, golfers have been somewhat slow to realize the benefits of training. Golf professionals from earlier generations believed there were negative implications from weight lifting and training. Thankfully that mindset has changed, and today you see players at all levels working out regularly. Jim and I believe when history looks at Tiger Woods, the single greatest impact he will have had on the game will be his introduction of weight training and fitness. You can see the results already in today's tour professionals such as David Duval, who re-sculpted his physique, and Colin Montgomery and Rocco Mediate who shed nearly 100 pounds between them. They knew that in order to compete with Tiger, and the next generation of golfers, they would have to be in much better shape.

The average recreational golfer is still hoping to purchase improvements to his game by buying clubs with new technol-

ogy, or "juiced" balls, or glomming onto the hot tip of the day. While the right equipment and proper instruction is necessary, so too is fitness. The golf ball will not respond if you cannot generate the proper clubhead speed. The average player will stay average if he is too weak, heavy, or lacks flexibility.

While some believe golf is slow-paced, in fact it requires strength, flexibility, stamina and skill. To play successfully, there are three components of fitness that you should develop: cardiovas-cular (aerobic) endurance; strength, and flexibility. These are the basis of any well-rounded fitness program.

Aerobic exercise: Gary Player, now in his fifth decade as a championship-level golfer, was the first professional golfer to fully appreciate the benefits of outstanding physical conditioning. He was a great believer in aerobic exercise, and understood its main purpose was to improve the cardio-respiratory system and help promote muscle tone. Another benefit of aerobic exercise is that it

Weight training: The two basic types of weight training are free weights and machines. Your program will vary depending upon your needs, but you should strive for high repetitions with fairly light weights rather than heavy weights with few repetitions. You are not trying to build bulky muscles, but long, supple ones. Your goal should be to increase strength without losing flexibility. A strength-training program should be done 2-3 days per week, with at least one set of 8-15 repetitions.

Hand strength: A frequently overlooked factor in achieving distance is hand strength. You create power with your swing, and that power is most efficiently transmitted if your hands are strong. This doesn't mean you should have a "death grip" on the club handle.

reduces psychological stress, and helps the player handle tournament pressure.

The three important characteristics of exercise are:

Frequency: You should exercise three to five times per week.

Duration: At least 15 minutes per session, but the best gains are achieved when the duration is extended to 30 to 60 minutes.

Intensity: You should strive for a heart rate increase that will test you—typically over 130 for an average male—but not exhaust you before your desired duration is achieved.

Best exercises: Cross country skiing, swimming, running, cycling, walking. You may want to first check with your health professional before starting any form of exercise.

Your grip pressure should be medium-soft. Sam Snead used to say he didn't have any calluses because he held the club as if it were a live bird in his hands and he wanted to apply just enough pressure so that bird couldn't fly away, but not so tightly that the bird couldn't breathe. If you have a proper grip , and hold the club this way you, too, will minimize calluses.

There is a direct correlation between hand strength and distance, and you can build your hand strength by exercising with a rubber ball, or hand exerciser made from a putty-type material. If there is a big difference in strength between your two hands, exercise your weaker hand more so the two are eventually close to equal. You can dramatically increase hand strength in a short period of time, which will add yards to your game.

Flexibility: This is the last component to developing a full and fluid swing. Here you can increase your range of motion in your shoulders, trunk, lower back, legs, arms, and hands with five minutes of stretching each day. Make sure that prior to stretching you spend a few minutes warming up your muscles to guard against strain or injury.

On Course Stretching and Flexibility Program

Achilles' Tendon/Shoulder Combination:

Stand with right foot forward, left foot behind and to the side.

Bend knee of left foot until you feel stretch on back of leg.

Cross right arm in front of shoulders and hold above elbow with left hand.

Hold for 12 seconds.

Switch feet and hold for 12 seconds.

Calf Stretch

Stand backwards with balls of feet on step—hold onto rail.

Have heels hang over step, lower heels as far as possible.

Hold for 12 seconds.

Chest Stretch:

Grasp vertical post of cart with right hand—keep arm at shoulder height and straight.

Turn body away until you feel a gentle stretch across chest.

Hold for 12 seconds.

Switch arms and repeat with left arm for 12 seconds.

Hamstrings Stretch:

Place left heel on seat of cart with knee slightly bent.

Bend forward from hips until you feel stretch in back of leg.

Hold for 12 seconds.

Switch legs and hold for 12 seconds with right heel on seat.

Back Stretch:

Face cart and grasp vertical post with both hands.

Straighten arms and gently bend from hips, keeping back straight toward cart.

When chest is parallel to the ground hold position for 12 seconds.

Quads Stretch:

Hold vertical post of cart with left hand.

Grasp right ankle with right hand and gently bring heel toward buttocks.

Stand tall.

Hold position for 12 seconds.

Switch to right hand on cart and left heel raised.

Hold for 12 seconds.

Triceps Stretch:

    Lift left arm up and bend elbow so left hand goes behind neck (spine).

    Gently grasp left elbow with right hand.

    Gently pull left elbow down.

    Hold for 12 seconds.

    Switch and stretch right arm with left hand.

    Hold for 12 seconds.

Rotator Cuff Stretch:

    Hold left upper arm across chest.

    Hold left arm just above chest.

    Gently push toward chest.

    Hold for 12 seconds.

    Switch to right arm across chest with left hand just above elbow.

    Gently push toward chest.

    Hold for 12 seconds.

Side Bends:

    Stand straight, feet hip width apart, and rest a long club across your shoulders, behind your head.

    Bend to right side from your hips, trying to touch your right elbow to your right hip.

    Repeat to left side.

    Repeat right and left for 12 cycles.

Twists:

Stand in address position with a long club resting across your shoulders behind your head.

Rotate trunk of body 90 degrees, with chest facing away from target, and shift weight to rear foot.

Rotate trunk forward, turning chest toward target.

Finish with weight on front foot, back heel up.

Have head in level position, looking at target.

Repeat 12 times slowly and smoothly.

Forearms:

Extend left arm out in front of body with elbow straight.

Hold palm away with fingers pointing up.

Gently pull left hand back to face with right palm.

Hold for 12 seconds.

Switch and repeat for right forearm. Hold for 12 seconds.

Wrists:

Extend left arm out in front of body with elbow straight.

Make a fist, turn knuckles down toward ground and hold for 12 seconds.

Turn knuckles up and hold for 12 seconds.

Repeat for right wrist, up and down. Hold for 12 seconds each way.

Etiquette

Etiquette is the way golfers act and dress on the golf course. Good etiquette will not lower your score, but it will make your experience more fun as well as make it more pleasant for your playing partners.

Dress: Many golf courses have dress codes that consist of comfortable clothes you probably already have.

Men and boys should wear: collared shirts, pants or shorts within 3" of the knee; and spikeless golf shoes, rubber-soled shoes, or sneakers.

Women and girls should wear: collared shirts or a "dressy" T-shirt; pants, skirts, or shorts within 3" of the knee; spikeless golf shoes, rubber-soled shoes, or sneakers.

Men and boys should not wear jeans tank tops or T-shirts, and women and girls should not wear jeans or halter tops.

Arrive early. At most courses you will have called ahead for a "starting" or "tee" time. Arrive at the course about an hour before that time so you can check in, pay, and most important warm up at the driving range and on the practice green. Check with the "starter" about 10 minutes before your assigned time. The starter will likely give you information such as the local rules, car policies, etc.

Warm-up. Put a club behind your back and rotate your body similarly to the way you would during the swing. Assume a stance similar to you normal address position. Rotate your backswing position and hold that position for 10 seconds. You will feel the "wind-up" that will create power. Then rotate your body to your follow-through position and again hold it for 10 seconds. It is not how fast you stretch, or how many times, but how fully you stretch. Do it slowly, and gradually you will increase you flexibility. The result will be increased distance.

Warm up shots. The best way to warm up is to start with short shots using a pitching wedge. Hit the first few with the goal of solid contact. Now pick a target. Gradually hit some longer irons, starting with an 8 iron, then a 5 iron, and work your way to your driver. With each shot, try to picture the shot you want to hit.

Visualize each shot and take this time to review your fundamentals: grip, posture, stance, alignment, address, rhythm and tempo. End the warm-up with a few short wedge shots so you leave the practice tee feeling confident about your swing.

First tee etiquette. Introduce yourself to strangers, and identify the ball you are playing. Play the appropriate tees. There are typically three sets: red is short, white is medium, and blue is long.

General course etiquette. Play ready golf, and be ready to hit when it is your turn. Yell "fore" if a ball you hit has even a slight chance of hitting someone. Stand to the side and slightly behind the player who is hitting. Play away if you are the farthest from the hole.

Pace of play. You should be able to play 18 holes in about four hours. To keep the game moving: minimize practice swings; play ready golf; move to your ball as soon as possible; try to keep up

106

Placing a club behind your back and imitating the action of a regular swing is a great way to loosen up.

with the group ahead of you; pick up if you have already hit a double par (twice the par on the hole) and move onto the next hole. Be ready

Care of the course. You should try to leave the course in better condition than you found it. You can do this by replacing all divots, fixing ball marks, raking sand traps, and showing general care of the course.

On-the-green etiquette. Mark your ball by placing a small coin or ball marker behind it. Repair ball marks on the green (yours and others). Repair a ball mark by using a tee or a divot tool to pry up the indentation made after the ball's impact. After you pry up the ball mark, tamp it down with the head of your putter.

Avoid walking in your playing partner's line (the imaginary path on the green directly between the ball and the hole.)

Look at your putt when other players are putting so you are ready when it's your turn.

Leave the green immediately after the hole has been completed.

Golf cart etiquette. Never drive close to greens or tees. Observe local course rules regarding where you can drive. Park at the exit toward the next tee.

Courtesy and common sense. Golf is a social game. Everyone in the foursome should have the opportunity to play without any unnecessary interference. The etiquette suggestions in this chapter cover most golf course protocol, but the single most important ingredient is common sense. Suggestions like staying still when one of the other players swings or keeping pace with the group ahead of you are normal courtesies that increase everyone's enjoyment.

Safety. Occasionally you may encounter lightning. When this happens, seek a building protected against being struck. Seek shelter in low lying areas, and avoid open fields, isolated trees and water.

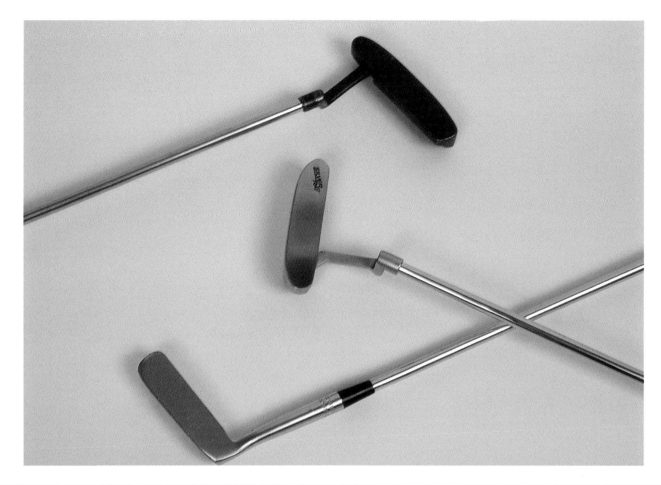

Some Rules

Golf has been played since the mid-1400s. For the first three hundred years there were no rules. In 1744, the Company of Gentlemen Golfers, Edinburgh, Scotland, wrote "The Original Rules of Golf." The three basic ideas behind the original rules were:

Play the ball as it lies.
Play the course as you find it.
When you cannot do either of these, do what is fair.

These ideas are still the foundation of the rules to this day. If you follow the spirit of these original rules you will be an honest golfer.

Golf is the only game with no umpires or referees. Golfers play by The Rules of Golf which are established by the United States Golf Association and the Royal and Ancient Golf Club of St. Andrews, Scotland. In tournament play, a rules official will help interpret the rules, but in both tournament and non-tournament lay it is up to the player to make decisions regarding the rules.

Scoring: There are two main types of play: match play and stroke play. Match play was the original form of play. In match play you play against one opponent and compete hole by hole. If player A scores a 6 on the first hole and player B scores a 4, then player B is "one up." The final score is determined by who wins the most holes. For instance, if player B has won 6 more holes than player A after 13 holes, then player A wins the match 6 and 5. Player B is 6 holes "up" with only 5 to play.

The other method of play is stroke or medal play. The medal score is simply the amount of strokes a player takes for the round of golf. This is the style of competition used most in professional tournaments. You play the course as do fellow competitors and the lowest score wins.

Rules: USGA Rule 13-1 says: "The ball shall be played as it lies, except as provided in the Rules." Following are a few circumstances where the ball is not played as it lies.

Lost ball. If you lose your ball you replay from the original position under a penalty of one stroke plus the original stroke.

Unplayable ball. If your ball lands in a spot you can't play from, you may move the ball under penalty of one stroke. You are the sole judge to determine if the ball is playable. You have three options, and you should choose the one that gives you the best relief:

You may drop a ball within two club lengths of the spot where the ball lay, but not nearer the hole.

You may drop a ball behind the spot where the ball lay, keeping that spot between you and the hole. There is no limit to how far back you can go.

You can exercise the same penalty for a lost ball, which is stroke and distance.

Water hazards. A water hazard (yellow stakes) is any sea, lake, pond, river, ditch, or anything similar. If you choose not to play from the hazard you may either drop another ball behind the hazard, under penalty of one stroke, keeping the point where the ball last crossed the margin of the hazard between yourself and the hole, or use the same procedure for a lost ball. Some water hazards are lateral (red stakes). If your ball goes in a lateral hazard you may drop a ball within two club lengths of where the ball last crossed the margin of the hazard, not nearer the hole, or a point on the opposite side of the hazard the same distance from the hole. You may also use the regular water hazard options. The penalty is one stroke.

Man-made objects. You get relief from man-made objects with no penalty. If your ball comes to rest next to a building (an immovable obstruction) you may take the nearest relief not nearer to the hole. If the ball comes to rest under a bench (a movable obstruction) you may move the bench.

Unfair conditions. There are some natural conditions that occur that are unfair and the rules provide relief.

"Ground Under Repair" is an area that is being worked on by the golf maintenance staff. This area is normally marked and defined by a painted white line.

A hole made by a burrowing animal.

Casual water, which is an accumulation of water.

In all three situations drop the ball within one club length of the nearest spot that provides relief, not nearer the hole. There is no penalty.

It is a good idea to buy a USGA Rules Book and carry it in your golf bag.

Some rules of golf are strange. If you whiff your tee shot—that is, swing and miss the ball completely—you will likely be embarrassed, and are charged one stroke. However, if you cream your drive 320 yards but it ends up an inch out of bounds, your penalty is stroke and distance, and you must play your next shot from the tee. Basically a two-stroke penalty for what was almost a wonderful drive.

Final Thoughts

This book was not designed to be the definitive text on golf, but a starting point. Read widely on the game, and learn as much as you can. Many of the fundamentals are the same, but each teacher and player has his own unique perspective on what works.

Golfers all want to consistently hit the ball with a solid, repeating swing. The key to consistency is balance, and anyone who performs a physical act that appears graceful is in balance.

Keep it simple: You can easily become very confused about the mechanics of your golf swing. A quick-fix gimmick will often create another problem in your swing that will lead to another compensation, and so on, and so on. When in doubt, stick to the proven fundamentals—they always work.

Find a good teacher: The PGA and LPGA set high standards for teachers, and you should find one with whom you are comfortable. You need not see your

teacher often, but maybe just a few times a year for a "check-up." The key is to not wait for your game to fall apart before you look for professional help, because it makes it harder for both you and the teacher. It's a good idea to take a lesson when you're playing well, because it's the ideal time to take your game to the next level.

Play at a good pace: Always play "ready golf," and be ready to hit as soon as it is your turn. As your playing partners are playing their shots, you should be lining up yours. Playing at a fairly quick pace makes the game more enjoyable for everyone, and you are more likely to stay mentally tuned in. Also, remember, not many slow players are asked to join foursomes.

Tinker on the range: When you are playing, focus on visualizing your shot, and don't worry about swing mechanics. Save tinkering with your swing for the range, and don't try to work on swing changes on the course.

Have fun: Remember why you're spending time playing golf. Don't make it work, and it will stay fun. Jim and I believe a bad day on the golf course beats a good day in the office. Have fun, and good luck.

Glossary

Ace A hole scored in one stroke.

Addressing the ball A player has addressed the ball when he has taken his stance by placing his feet in position for, and in preparation of, making a stroke and has also grounded his club. In a hazard a player has addressed the ball when he has taken his stance in preparation of making a stroke.

Albatross Term used in Britain for a score of three under the par for a hole. In the United States this score is known as a double-eagle.

All Square An even score, neither side being a hole up.

Approach A shot to the putting green.

Apron The last few yards of fairway in front of the green.

Away The ball that is farthest from the hole.

Back Nine Second set of nine holes on an 18-hole golf course.

Balata Natural or synthetic compound used to make the cover for top-standard golf balls. Its soft, elastic qualities produce a high spin rate. A ball favored by tournament players.

Backspin Backward rotation of the ball, causing it to stop abruptly.

Bent Grass Type of fine-leafed grass that produces an ideal surface for putting greens. It is, however, difficult to maintain in hot climates.

Best Ball Match in which a single player competes against the best ball of two or more.

Birdie Term used for a score of one under the par for a hole.

Blind An approach position from which the green cannot be seen.

Bogey Term used for a score of one over the par for a hole.

Borrow British term for the amount a putt will deviate from a straight line due to the slope of the putting green.

Break American term for the amount a putt will deviate from a straight line due to the slope of the putting green.

Bunker An area of bare ground, often a marked depression, usually covered with sand.

Bye Holes Holes remaining after a match is finished, that is, after one side is more holes up than remain for play.

Caddie A person who carries the player's clubs.

Carry Distance between the point from which a ball is played to the point where it lands. When the ball is hit over water or a bunker, it is said to "carry" the hazard.

Casual Water Any temporary accumulation of water, such as a puddle after rain.

Cavity-Back Iron Clubhead designed with the weight on the periphery of the head to create a larger sweet spot.

Chip Low running shot normally played from near the edge of the green toward the hole.

Concede To grant that an opponent has won a hole before play has been completed.

Cross bunker Bunker lying across the line of the fairway.

Cup The hole into which the ball is played, 4 1/2 inches in diameter and at least 4 inches deep.

Cut To miss the cut is to fail to score low enough, usually over the first 36 holes of a 72-tournament, to qualify for the final two rounds.

Cut Shot Shot that makes the ball spin in a clockwise direction, resulting in a left-to-right bending flight. It can be either deliberate or a mistake.

Default To concede a match to an opponent without playing against him; to fail to appear for a scheduled match.

Divot A piece of turf cut out by a club during a stroke. Divots should always be replaced before the player moves on.

Dogleg A hole that changes direction midway through, normally in the landing area for the tee-shot. It can either bend to left or right.

Dormie Term used in matchplay for the situation in which a player or team is leading by as many holes as there are left to play and therefore cannot be beaten.

Double-eagle Term used in the United States for three under the par for a hole. In Britain this score is known as an albatross.

Down In match play, a side is down when it has lost more holes than it has won.

Draw A stroke deliberately played with right-to-left spin (for a right-handed player), which causes the ball to curve from right to left in its flight. An uncontrolled draw becomes a hook.

Draw Method that decides who plays against whom in a matchplay competition, or a group of fellow competitors playing a strokeplay competition. Whoever is drawn first has the honor of playing the first on the opening tee.

Driver Club with a long shaft and little loft used for driving the ball the maximum distance from the tee.

Dub An unskillful player; also, to hit the ball poorly.

Eagle Term that denotes a score of two under the par for a hole.

Face Slope of a bunker; part of the club head that strikes the ball.

Fade Stroke deliberately played with left-to-right spin (for a right-handed player) that causes the ball to curve from left-to-right in its flight. An uncontrolled fade becomes a slice.

Fairway Area of closely mowed turf that lays between tee and green, which has as its boundary either longer grass known as semirough or completely uncut grass called rough.

Feathery Early type of golf ball made by filling a leather pouch with boiled feathers. It was highly susceptible to damage and began to go out of use in the mid-1880s after the introduction of the cheaper guttie ball.

Flagstick Movable straight indicator, usually a lightweight pole with a numbered flag, placed in the hole to show its location; sometimes referred to as the pin.

Fluffy Lie Situation in which the ball finishes suspended in rough grass slightly above the ground. In Britain, this is called a perched lie.

Follow-through Continuation of the swing of the club after the ball has been struck.

"Fore!" Warning cry by a player to any person in the way of his ball.

Forecaddie A person employed to indicate the position of balls on the course.

Fourball Match involving four players in teams of two, in which each player plays his own ball.

Foursome Four golfers playing together, or a match involving four players in teams of two, in which each team plays one ball by alternate strokes. At the start of play each team decides which player will play the first tee-shot, after which they alternate the tee-shot on each hole.

Free Drop Ball that is dropped without penalty away from an immovable obstruction, or in other circumstances, in accordance with the Rules of Golf.

Front Nine First nine holes on an 18-hole golf course.

Graphite (carbon fiber) Carbon-based substance that, when bonded in layers, produces an exceptionally strong but very light material ideal for golf-club shafts. It is increasingly used also in the manufacture of clubheads.

Great Triumvirate Name given collectively to the three outstanding British professionals who dominated golf before World War I: James Braid, J.H. Taylor and Harry Vardon.

Green Area of mowed grass specially prepared for putting, into which the hole is cut. It is separated from the fairway by the "apron," a fringe of grass longer than the green but shorter than the fairway. Originally the term "green" was used for a whole course.

Gross A player's score before deducting any handicap.

Ground To sole or rest the club lightly on the ground, in preparing to strike the ball.

Ground Under Repair Any portion of the course under repair or maintenance. If a ball should land on ground under repair or if the ground under repair should interfere with the players stance or swing, the ball may be lifted an dropped, without penalty, as near as possible to where it lay, but not nearer the hole.

Guttie Ball introduced in 1848, made of gutta percha a rubberlike substance obtained from the latex of a Malaysian tree species.

Halved A hole is halved when each side has taken the same number of strokes.

Handicap System that subtracts strokes from the scores of weaker players to enable people of varying abilities to play against one another on theoretically equal terms. The handicap is usually based on the average scores of a player set against a standard for a course.

Hanging Lie Situation in which the ball rests on a slope running away from the player.

Hazard Any bunker or water hazard.

Heel Part of the clubhead nearest the shaft.

Hole General term for the whole region between tee and green, but also means the specific target in the ground. It has a standard diameter of 4 1/2 in. (10.8 cm). See cup.

Hole out Make the final stroke in playing the ball into the hole.

Hook Stroke that bends sharply to the left, (for the right-handed player) caused by the application of counterclockwise spin, either deliberately or unintentionally.

Hosel Socket on an iron-headed club that serves to connect the iron clubhead to the shaft.

Interlocking Grip Method of gripping the handle of the club in which the little finger of the right hand intertwines with the forefinger of the left hand (the opposite applies for a left-handed player). It is usually favored by players with small hands or short fingers to maintain a firm grip.

Lie Situation in which a ball finishes after completion of a stroke. The lie can vary from good to bad, depending on how far the ball has settled down in the grass or, in the case of a bunker, in the sand.

Line The direction in which a player desires his ball to travel.

Links Stretch of ground beside the sea upon which golf is played. Linksland is usually low-lying, with sand dunes supporting fine, salt-resistant grasses. The word probably derives from the fact that linksland links the shoreline and agricultural land farther from the sea.

Loft Angle of slope of a face of a club away from the vertical. The loft increases with the number of the iron, giving a higher flight trajectory and less distance.

Long Game The strokes where attaining distance is the most important factor.

Loose Impediments Natural object not fixed or growing, as a stone, leaf or twig.

LPGA Acronym for Ladies' Professional Golf Association.

Marker A scorer in stroke play appointed by a tournament committee to record a competitor's score; a marker indicating the front edge of a teeing ground or the boundaries of a hole.

Match Play Form of competition in which the number of holes won or lost by a player or team, rather than the number of strokes taken, determines the winner. The alternative and more common competition in the professional game is Stroke Play.

Medal Play Alternative name for stroke-play.

Nassau A system of scoring under which one point is awarded for winning the first 9 holes, one for the second 9, and a third for the full 18.

Net Score after deducting handicap.

Observer Person appointed by a tournament committee to assist a referee in deciding questions of fact and to report to him any breach of a rule or a local rule.

Obstruction Anything artificial that has been erected, placed, or left on the course.

Out-of-bounds Ground on which play is prohibited.

Overlapping grip Another name for the Vardon grip.

Par Theoretically perfect play, or the score an expert would be expected to make on a hole, calculated on the number of strokes required to reach the green plus two putts. Par is calculated on the basis of distance. Women's par for a course is slightly higher than par for men. USGA standards for computing par are:

	Men's Par	Women's Par
Par 3	up to 250 yd.	up to 210 yd.
Par 4	251 to 470 yd.	211 to 400 yd.
Par 5	471 and over	401 to 575 yd.
Par 6		576 yd. and over

Penalty Stroke A stroke added to the score of a player under certain rules.

Perched Lie Situation in which the ball finishes suspended in rough grass slightly above the ground. In the United States, this is called a fluffy lie.

PGA Acronym for the Professional Golfers' Association.

Pin A rod or pole to which a flag is attached (see Flagstick).

Pin High A ball is said to be "pin high" on the green when it has been played as far as the placement of the hole and any distance either side. It is also known as hole high.

Pitch An approach on which the ball is lofted in a high arc (see Chip).

Pitch-and-Run An approach on which a part of the desired distance is covered by the roll of the ball after it strikes the ground.

Pivot The turn of the body as a stroke is played.

Plugged Lie Situation in which a ball remains in the indentation or plug mark it makes when it lands. Except under a local rule that permits a plugged ball to be lifted and moved (but not nearer the hole) without penalty, a plugged ball must be played as it lies.

Plus Handicap A handicap less than the scratch score of the course. Plus handicap players have strokes added to their score because they regularly beat the standard scratch score in match play.

Pot Bunker Small, round, and deep bunker commonly found on traditional British links courses, most famously on the Old Course at St. Andrews.

Pull To hit the ball so that it will curve to the left (for the right-handed player).

Putt Stroke made on a putting green.

Putting Green All ground of the hole being played that is specially prepared for putting or is otherwise defined as such by the committee.

R&A Acronym for the Royal & Ancient Golf Club of St. Andrews—the governing body of golf in all countries except for the United States and Mexico.

Ready Golf Playing swiftly and being prepared to hit as soon as it is your turn.

Referee Person appointed by the tournament committee to accompany players to decide questions of fact and rules of golf.

Rough Long grass bordering the fairway, also at times between tee and fairway; may include bushes, trees, etc.

Run To run a ball along the ground in an approach instead of chipping or pitching it; distance a ball rolls after it lands.

Sand Trap A bunker having a layer of sand (see Bunker).

Sand Wedge Extremely lofted club, also known as a "sand iron," with a wide flange designed for playing from bunkers. The wide flange "bounces" the clubhead through the sand. Gene Sarazen is credited with its invention.

Scratch Description of a golfer whose handicap equals that of the scratch score of the course. The scratch player gives strokes to all players with a higher handicap and receives strokes from players who have plus handicaps.

Shank Badly mis-hit stroke in which the ball is usally struck with the hosel or socket of an iron-headed club.

Short Game Approach shots and putts.

Single Match between two players.

Slice Shot carrying considerable clockwise spin that consequently curves violently to the right (for the right-handed player).

Slot Ideal position at the top of the back-swing in which the club is set ready for the downswing.

Splash Stroke from a bunker in which the sand wedge enters the sand before the ball and carries it out of the bunker on a cushion of sand.

Square When a match is even.

Stroke Play Form of competition in which the number of strokes a player takes to complete a round is compared with the other players' scores for a round.

Stance The position of a player's feet and body when addressing the ball.

Stroke Hole Hole on which a handicap stroke is given.

Stroke Play has largely supplanted the traditional Match Play form in professional tournament golf.

Stymie Situation in which one player's ball blocked another player's ball's route to the hole. The stymied player was required to play over the top of the offending ball. The stymie was outlawed in 1951 by the USGA and the R&A.

Surlyn™ Trademark of a thermoplastic resin similar to natural balata, used in ball manufacture. It is an extremely resilient material and virtually indestructible by clubs.

Sweet Spot Precise point on the face of a golf club, usually in the center, that will deliver the maximum possible mass behind the ball. A ball struck at this point will travel farther than one struck on any other part of the face.

Tee Closely mowed area from which the first stroke on a hole is played. The term is also used to refer to the tee peg.

Three Ball Match Match in which three play against one another, each playing his own ball.

Threesome Match in which one player competes against two, who play alternate strokes with the same ball.

Topped Stroke in which the club strikes the top of the ball, causing it to run along the ground.

Up and Down Approach shot and a single putt from anywhere off the green. Usually refers to holing out in two shots from a bunker or from just off the green.

USGA Acronym for the United States Golf Association—the governing body for golf in the United States and Mexico.

Vardon Grip Method of holding the handle of the club in which the little finger of the right hand overlaps the forefinger of the left (the opposite applies for left-handed players). Popularized, but not invented by Harry Vardon, it is also known as the overlapping grip.

Water Hazard Any water (except casual water) on the course.

Yips Nervous disorder that can destroy a player's ability to putt, turning the stroke into a twitching or jerking movement.

Bibliography

The Inner Game of Golf, W. Timothy Gallwey

The Inner Game of Tennis, W. Timothy Gallwey

Five Modern Lessons, Ben Hogan

Power Golf, Ben Hogan

Exercise Guide to Golf, Frank Jobe

"The Mental Hazards of Golf," <u>Vanity Fair</u>, 1929, Bobby Jones

Bobby Jones on Golf, Bobby Jones

The Fundamentals of Hogan, David Leadbetter

Golf and the Kingdom, Michael Murphy

Golf My Way, Jack Nicklaus

Little Red Book, Harvey Penick

Hogan, Curt Sampson

GOLF CLUB EQUIPMENT & PLAYING EVALUATION

FITTING SCORE CARD

CIRCLE PAR 3's
SQUARE PAR 5's

CIRCLE WOODS AND IRONS BELOW TO SHOW YOUR SET MAKEUP

Column header labels (angled):
Fairways Hit (H) / Missed Left (L) Right (R)
Greens Hit (H) Regulation / Missed Left (L) Right (R) / Short (S) Over (O)
Greenside Bunkers / Hit (H), Out & 1 Putt (1) / Out & 2 Putts (2)
Number of Putts / 1, 2, 3, or 4
Total Shots Per Hole

HOLE	WOODS 1	2	3	4	5	6	7	IRONS 1	2	3	4	5	6	7	8	9	PW	SW	3W	Fairway	Green	Bunker	Putts	Score
1																				H L R	H L R S O	H 1 2	1 2 3 4	
2																				H L R	H L R S O	H 1 2	1 2 3 4	
3																				H L R	H L R S O	H 1 2	1 2 3 4	
4																				H L R	H L R S O	H 1 2	1 2 3 4	
5																				H L R	H L R S O	H 1 2	1 2 3 4	
6																				H L R	H L R S O	H 1 2	1 2 3 4	
7																				H L R	H L R S O	H 1 2	1 2 3 4	
8																				H L R	H L R S O	H 1 2	1 2 3 4	
9																				H L R	H L R S O	H 1 2	1 2 3 4	
OUT																								
HOLE	1	2	3	4	5	6	7	1	2	3	4	5	6	7	8	9	PW	SW	3W	Fairway	Green	Bunker	Putts	Score
10																				H L R	H L R S O	H 1 2	1 2 3 4	
11																				H L R	H L R S O	H 1 2	1 2 3 4	
12																				H L R	H L R S O	H 1 2	1 2 3 4	
13																				H L R	H L R S O	H 1 2	1 2 3 4	
14																				H L R	H L R S O	H 1 2	1 2 3 4	
15																				H L R	H L R S O	H 1 2	1 2 3 4	
16																				H L R	H L R S O	H 1 2	1 2 3 4	
17																				H L R	H L R S O	H 1 2	1 2 3 4	
18																				H L R	H L R S O	H 1 2	1 2 3 4	
IN																								
TOTAL																								

NAME _____
COURSE _____
PAR _____
DATE _____
HDCP _____

©1985 Ralph Maltby Enterprises, Inc.

INSTRUCTIONS:
- Fill Card Out on Next Tee while Others in Your Group Hit
- Place an "X" in Woods and Irons Section to Indicate Clubs Hit on Each Hole
- Circle any "X" to Indicate any Unsolid Feeling Hit, Regardless of the Result
- Square Any "X" to Indicate a Chip Shot
- Circle Appropriate Letters and/or Numbers in Fairway, Green, Bunker & Putts Column
- At Bottom of "Putts" Column, in the "Total" Block, Write in Total Putts for the Round

COMMENTS: _____
_____
_____
_____
_____

About The Authors

Jay Morelli, Vice President of Golf for Mount Snow, Ltd., has been teaching and improving golfers at all skill levels for more than 35 years. He founded The *Original* Golf School™ and The Accelerated Teaching Method™ in June 1978. With more than 80,000 alumni, The *Original* Golf School™ is the largest and oldest in the country and annually graduates 5,000 students. Golf Digest voted him the top teaching pro in Vermont. He has been named New England PGA Teacher-of-the-Year, Vermont PGA Pro-of-the-Year, has won the New England PGA Bill Strasbaugh Award, is a New York PGA Section Champion, a multiple Vermont Pro-Pro Champion, and was head professional at several private clubs. He has produced four major videos. This is his second book. He has a BA from Florida State University.

Jim Reichert is a publisher, book packager, literary agent, and has written and published books on topics ranging from golf to personal finance. He has a B.A. from Miami University, an M.A. from Washington University, and an M.G.A. from Penn. When he was younger, he played golf to a 2-handicap. Now that he spends the bulk of his free time chasing after his two young children, it's quite safe to say he's no longer a 2.

Bruce Curtis has chronicled many of the significant events of the last decades as a photographer for Time, Life and Sports Illustrated. His work has taken him from the jungles of Vietnam to ringside with Ali and Frazier, to the White House. He has been featured in dozens upon dozens of books, magazines and advertisements. You can view his work at www.beenthereshotthat.com.